Yoga

Yoga

BARBARA SHEEN

LUCENT BOOKS

A part of Gale, Cengage Learning

GALE
CENGAGE Learning·

Farmington Hills, Mich • San Francisco • New York • Waterville, Maine
Meriden, Conn • Mason, Ohio • Chicago

LIBRARY OF CONGRESS CATALOGING-IN-PUBLICATION DATA

Sheen, Barbara.
Yoga / by Barbara Sheen.
   pages cm. -- (Science behind sports)
Includes glossary.
Includes bibliographical references and index.
ISBN 978-1-4205-1229-8 (hardcover)
1. Yoga--Juvenile literature. 2. Yoga--Health aspects--Juvenile literature.
3. Sports science--Juvenile literature. I. Title.
  RA781.7.S4467 2014
  613.7'046--dc23
                     2014020478

Lucent Books
27500 Drake Rd
Farmington Hills MI 48331

ISBN-13: 978-1-4205-1229-8
ISBN-10: 1-4205-1229-3

Printed in the United States of America
1 2 3 4 5 6 7 18 17 16 15 14

CONTENTS

FOREWORD

On March 21, 1970, Slovenian ski jumper Vinko Bogataj took a terrible fall while competing at the Ski-flying World Championships in Oberstdorf, West Germany. Bogataj's pinwheeling crash was caught on tape by an ABC *Wide World of Sports* film crew and eventually became synonymous with "the agony of defeat" in competitive sporting. While many viewers were transfixed by the severity of Bogataj's accident, most were not aware of the biomechanical and environmental elements behind the skier's fall—heavy snow and wind conditions that made the ramp too fast and Bogataj's inability to maintain his center of gravity and slow himself down. Bogataj's accident illustrates that, no matter how mentally and physically prepared an athlete may be, scientific principles—such as momentum, gravity, friction, and aerodynamics—always have an impact on performance.

Lucent Books' Science Behind Sports series explores these and many more scientific principles behind some of the most popular team and individual sports, including baseball, hockey, gymnastics, wrestling, swimming, and skiing. Each volume in the series focuses on one sport or group of related sports. The volumes open with a brief look at the featured sport's origins, history and changes, then move on to cover the biomechanics and physiology of playing, related health and medical concerns, and the causes and treatment of sports-related injuries.

In addition to learning about the arc behind a curve ball, the impact of centripetal force on a figure skater, or how water buoyancy helps swimmers, Science Behind Sports readers will also learn how exercise, training, warming up, and diet and nutrition directly relate to peak performance and enjoyment of the sport. Volumes may also cover why certain sports are popular, how sports function in the business world, and which hot sporting issues—sports doping and cheating, for example—are in the news.

Basic physical science concepts, such as acceleration, kinetics, torque, and velocity, are explained in an engaging and accessible manner. The full-color text is augmented by fact boxes, sidebars, photos, and detailed diagrams, charts and graphs. In addition, a subject-specific glossary, bibliography, and index provide further tools for researching the sports and concepts discussed throughout Science Behind Sports.

CHAPTER 1

An Ancient Practice

Yoga is an ancient practice that began as a spiritual discipline in India more than four thousand years ago. For ancient yogis (male yoga practitioners), yoga was a means of achieving spiritual fulfillment. The goal of most modern yoga practitioners, on the other hand, focuses on improving their physical and mental well-being through the performance of physical postures known as *asanas* that are coordinated with conscious breathing. Breath control exercises, known as *pranayama*, and meditation are other components of modern yoga. As an article on the American Yoga Association's website explains:

The body is looked upon as the primary instrument that enables us to work and evolve in the world, and so a Yoga student treats it with great care and respect. Breathing techniques are based on the concept that breath is the source of life in the body. The Yoga student gently increases breath control to improve the health and function of both body and mind. The two systems of exercise and breathing then prepare the body and mind for meditation, and the student finds an easy approach to quiet the mind that allows silence and healing from everyday stress. Regular practice of all three parts of this structure of Yoga produces a clear, bright mind and a strong, capable body.[1]

Ancient Roots

The practice of yoga has changed considerably since it began. If an ancient yogi were alive today, he probably would be quite surprised at the transformation. Clay stamps depicting a male figure seated cross-legged in a posture associated with yogic meditation are the earliest evidence of yoga. The stamps, which were found in India, date back to about 2500 B.C. Since yoga was a male-only practice until the twentieth century, women are not depicted on any ancient yoga artifacts.

Ancient yogis were mystics who dedicated their lives to yoga. They believed that through yoga they could enter a trance-like state in which their bodies and minds could connect with the invisible spiritual world and join with a higher power. As a result, they would gain self-knowledge and spiritual enlightenment. In order to reach such a state, yogis had to be still and focus their minds inward, ignoring

A stone seal unearthed at Mohenjo-Daro (in present-day Pakistan) showing a buffalo-horned Shiva is the oldest known representation of yogic meditation. The seal is currently in the collection of the National Museum, New Delhi, in India.

all distractions, for long periods of time. According to author Georg Feuerstein, "Such inner focusing for the sake of transcending the limitations of the ordinary mind is the root of Yoga. When successful, the . . . yogi was graced with a 'vision' or experience of the transcendental [mystical or supernatural] reality."[2]

To avoid distractions, many yogis lived alone in isolated mountain caves. They experimented with stretching their bodies into different positions and manipulating their breathing in an effort to gain control of their minds and bodies so that they could enter a transcendental state. Through these efforts they learned about their breath, bodies, and minds, and the connection between them. As author Timothy McCall explains:

The ancient yogis didn't have fancy machines or advanced technology to study the internal organs or the nervous system. Instead, they used observational powers of the body itself. They manipulated the body in every way they could think of and experimented with various techniques for channeling the breath, and as they did this they explored the effects. They believed that what they learned about themselves helped them to better understand the world around them; the more they explored and observed, the more sophisticated their ability to perceive different aspects and subtleties of the body became.[3]

Through these experiments, they learned that concentrating on their breathing helped to clear their minds and direct their focus inward. They also learned that breathing slowly and deeply greatly relaxed them, which helped the yogis remain still for hours. Breathing rapidly, they observed, energized them. When rapid breathing was done repeatedly, it caused them to feel light-headed, and in extreme cases it caused them to hallucinate. Such hallucinations were often interpreted as spiritual visions.

The yogis did not know it then, but their observation about how their breathing affected their bodies and minds was rooted in science. Modern science has proved that slow, deep breathing has a calming effect on the body and mind. It decreases heart rate and blood pressure and eases feel-

A monk meditates inside a cave in Mellagalla, Sri Lanka, in 1954. Many yogis lived in isolated mountain caves to avoid distraction.

ings of anxiety, which is why when people are panicked they are told to take a deep breath. Science also has shown that fast breathing stimulates the muscles and nerves. Extreme fast breathing, known as hyperventilation, lowers the flow of oxygen to the brain, which can cause people to feel dizzy or pass out.

Some yogis became so skillful at breath control that they could slow their breathing and heart rate to the point where, to a casual observer, they appeared dead. Then, by breathing

MEDITATE

The word yoga—meaning to join, connect, unite, or become whole—comes from the ancient Indian language of Sanskrit.

rapidly, they could speed up their metabolism and appear to rise from the dead. Because of this ability, for a time, yogis were considered to possess magical powers. In reality, there was no magic involved. As Robert Rose, executive director of Chicago's MacArthur Foundation's Initiative on Mind, Brain, Body, and Health Research, explains, "Thousands of research studies have shown that in the practice of yoga a person can learn to control such physiologic parameters as blood pressure, heart rate, respiratory function, metabolic rate, skin resistance, brain waves and body temperature, among other body functions."[4]

Scientists explain the yogis' feats in two ways. First, whereas an average, relaxed person takes about fifteen breaths per minute, with practice, expert yogis could take one breath per minute. This produced a large build-up of carbon dioxide in their bodies, which drastically slowed their metabolism. In fact, animals breathe in this manner in preparation for hibernation. The yogis' breathing also shifted the balance in their autonomic nervous system, the part of the nervous system that regulates the function of organs such as the heart and lungs. The autonomic nervous system has two branches, the sympathetic nervous system, which helps the body face perceived emergencies, and the parasympathetic nervous system, which helps the body rest. Through slow breathing, the yogis stimulated the parasympathetic nervous system. It is responsible for relaxation. It lowers the heart rate and blood pressure, calms the nerves, and inhibits the release of adrenaline and cortisol, the hormones associated with stress.

The Yoga Sutras

Yoga practices were passed down through one-on-one oral teaching until the second century, when a yogi named Patanjali wrote the *Yoga Sutras,* a text that explains the discipline of yoga. In the *Yoga Sutras*, Patanjali describes yoga as a system of ethics and personal discipline, which, when followed, helps practitioners gain self-understanding, mental clarity, peace of mind, and ultimately spiritual enlightenment. To help yogis move along this path, Patanjali divided the practice of yoga into eight steps or components that progress from external concerns to internal or spiritual concerns. Since it was assumed that inexperienced yogis had a mentor to guide them, Patanjali provided little instruction on how to master each step.

Briefly, these are the eight components: The first component is *yama*, or a person's attitude to the environment. This includes protecting all living things and the earth. The second is *niyama*, or an individual's attitude toward the self. This includes maintaining personal cleanliness and good health habits. The third component is *asana*, or physical exercise. The fourth is *pranayama*, or the deliberate regulation of the breath. The fifth step is *pratyahara* or the restraint of the senses. It involves people being attentive to whatever they are doing. The sixth step is *dharana*, or meditation—that is, the ability to direct or focus the mind on a particular object, which may be concrete, an idea, or spiritual in nature. The seventh component is *dhyana*. It describes a deep meditative state in which individuals develop an understanding of the object of their focus. The final component, *samadhi*, or enlightenment, is the deepest meditative or trance-like state. Individuals who master samadhi lose their self-awareness and become one with the object they are focused upon. When the object focused upon in samadhi is spiritual in nature, a yogi is believed to have attained spiritual enlightenment.

Patanjali's system became known as Ashtanga or Royal (Raja) yoga. Other yoga systems also developed. Each had the same goal, spiritual enlightenment, but each emphasized different methods of obtaining it. These systems included Bhakti yoga, or the yoga of devotion, which is largely a spiritual practice; Jnana yoga, or the yoga of wisdom, which focuses on the study of religious and yoga texts; Karma yoga, or the yoga of action, which emphasizes living life in a selfless manner; Tantra or Kundalini yoga, or the yoga of continuity and relationships, which involves

Yogis and Magic

Most ancient yogis dedicated their life to practicing yoga. Consequently, they had no income and often showed off their "magical powers" in village fairs in exchange for food or money. Many of their magical powers were simple tricks based on their power of observation. For instance, they watched people carefully and listened to their conversations. Then they pretended to read people's minds based on what they had seen or heard. If they saw a man coming out of a doctor's office, when reading that person's mind they might say that the individual was worried about his health. They also pretended to tell fortunes. Knowing that people want to hear good things about the future, they might tell that same person that he would be feeling better soon and would live a long time.

They also performed illusions such as pretending to be buried alive. Usually these "burials" took places in small seemingly sealed caves or cells. The caves or cells, however, had a hidden hole from which the yogi could escape, mystifying onlookers with their reappearance.

performing specific rituals; and Hatha yoga, or the yoga of physical discipline. All of these yoga systems were influenced by the *Yoga Sutras.*

Hatha Yoga

Most popular forms of modern yoga have their roots in Hatha yoga, which was the only system to describe specific asanas, or yoga postures. Hatha means "forceful" in the ancient Indian language of Sanskrit. Hatha yoga focused on the third, fourth, and fifth components of the *Yoga Sutras*: physical exercise, breath control, and meditation as a way to achieve spiritual enlightenment. It took a holistic approach to yoga practice by concentrating on the connection between the body and the mind. Hatha yoga practitioners believed that the body contains passages called *nadis* through which *prana*, a vital fluid or life force, is channeled. They thought that any blockages in these passages impeded the flow of prana and negatively affected a person's state of mind. This made it impossible for yogis to focus their minds with sufficient intensity to achieve spiritual fulfillment. Such blockages, they professed, were caused by illness, stress, or other physical or emotional problems. To keep these channels open, they developed fifteen asanas, or physical exercises, breathing techniques, and meditation strategies. The combination, they said, resulted in practitioners obtaining physical and mental well-being. Although there is no scientific evidence that nadis or prana exist, science has shown that the body and mind are constantly interacting, and there is a very real health connection between the two. As McCall explains in an article in *Yoga Journal*:

> If you've ever felt the butterflies in the pit of your stomach as you prepared to make a presentation, you've felt how your thoughts affect the functioning of your intestines. An athlete who "chokes" at a big moment in a competition, performing worse than usual, is similarly seeing the results of a fearful state of mind on his or her ability to coordinate muscular actions. . . . It works the other way too. . . . On several occasions over the years, I have found myself feeling depressed for no reason I could apprehend. Only the next morning, when a sore throat, nasal congestion, and other flu symptoms had appeared, did I realize that my sour mood had been the way my mind was reacting to the impending illness (and my body's response to it), even though I had no conscious awareness of it.[5]

It is a proven fact that the mind can produce chemical changes in the body that affect physical health. It is not uncommon for people under severe stress to develop headaches, stomach ulcers, or high blood pressure. Stress has also been shown to affect digestion, cause

MEDITATE

12

Number of flowing yoga postures in the popular Sun Salutation sequence. The first book to describe it was written by Krishnamacharya.

heart palpitations, and weaken the immune system, making individuals more prone to catching colds and infections. Conversely, some mental illnesses are caused by biological factors such as a chemical imbalance and are treated with drugs that help rectify the imbalance. According to an article in *NIH Medline Plus*, a magazine published by the National Institute of Health:

> Today, we accept that there is a powerful mind-body connection through which emotional, mental, social, spiritual, and behavioral factors can directly affect our health. . . . Over the past 20 years, mind-body medicine has provided evidence that psychological factors can play a major role in such illnesses as heart disease, and that mind-body techniques can aid in their treatment.[6]

Indeed, the link between the mind and the body has been shown to be so strong that a new field of medicine known as integrative medicine has developed around it. When diagnosing and treating health problems, integrative medical professionals look at physical, emotional, and mental factors that affect a person's health.

Postural Yoga

Although Hatha yoga included specific postures, it was not until the early twentieth century that the idea of yoga as a fitness regime became popular. At that time, India was beginning to seek its independence from its colonial ruler, Great Britain. Yoga, with its roots in ancient India, was seen as an important part of India's national identity. It was also seen by Indian freedom fighters as a way to physically strengthen the Indian people should a violent struggle arise. As a result, emphasis began to be placed on the physical side of Hatha yoga. As this emphasis expanded, new forms of yoga developed along with interest in how yoga impacted health and its therapeutic effect.

Two men, Jagannath Gune, also known as Swami Kuvalayananda, and Tirumalai Krishnamacharya, also known as Krishna, were instrumental in changing yoga. Gune was one of the first people to connect science with yoga and to promote yoga as a fitness and health regime.

An Indian man practices postural yoga in 1940. The decades-long struggle for Indian independence in the early twentieth century also led to the creation of new forms of yoga.

He was an Indian physical fitness educator and a freedom fighter who was concerned with strengthening Indian youth. He established an *ashram*, or yoga retreat, with a laboratory where he investigated the effects of asanas and pranayama on the body. As part of his studies, he measured and compared the blood pressure, X-rays, and blood oxygen level of yogis before, during, and after they performed various yoga postures and breathing exercises. He published the results of his studies in a scientific journal he authored, which was distributed internationally. Based on the results of his studies, he recommended specific postures for particular health issues. For instance, he found that performing a headstand lowered blood pressure, so he recommended the practice to the Indian leader Mahatma Gandhi, who suffered from high blood pressure.

To reach as many people as possible, Gune's ashram offered large group yoga classes, which was a radical departure from the one-on-one instruction of the past. He also allowed women (known as yoginis) to attend the classes because he felt that females, too, needed to be strengthened. The idea of large co-ed yoga classes proved to be farsighted. Today, most people learn yoga in co-ed classes, and the majority of yoga practitioners in the United States are women.

Gune included new postures in the classes, which he adapted from Indian martial arts—a subject he studied as a youth. His method of performing yoga was very strengthening. He had students hold each posture for long periods while focusing on their breathing. Holding difficult postures in this manner is not easy. It takes strength and stamina. Instructing students to focus on their breathing helped them maintain the postures and to direct their attention inward.

Yoga pioneer B.K.S. Iyengar gives a yoga demonstration at a 1960 event in London, England.

Like Gune, Krishna was influenced by Indian martial arts. He was hired by an Indian royal family to start a yoga school to strengthen local youth. His classroom was a former gymnastics studio equipped with Indian and European gymnastics and wrestling manuals. Using the manuals as a guide, he adapted and developed yoga postures that incorporated gymnastic and wrestling exercises. He sequenced the postures so that one asana flowed into the next and combined them with deep breathing exercises. This was a more dynamic and graceful way of doing yoga than Gune's method. It became the basis for many modern styles of yoga.

Spreading the Word

Both Gune and Krishna trained a number of individuals who later became influential in bringing yoga practice to the West. These individuals developed their own styles of yoga based on Gune's and Krishna's teaching. Among these yoga pioneers was B.K.S. Iyengar. Iyengar was a sickly young man who began studying yoga in hopes of improving his health. As he gained strength, he became interested in how yoga practice could be adapted for people with different levels of agility or strength. He adapted and/or developed more than two hundred different yoga postures and fourteen breathing exercises based on careful study of human anatomy. He also developed a number of yoga props such as belts and blocks, which helped students of all skill levels to extend their reach so that they could safely perform difficult postures. As author William J. Broad explains:

> Intimate knowledge of the human body—such as how its more than two hundred bones fit together and fall into conflict—let Iyengar refine the poses. . . . His method avoided subtle misalignments that could restrict movement. . . . Iyengar became a master of precision. Good alignment became his signature. He learned much about what was reasonable, what was ambitious, and what was dangerous.[7]

Iyengar's style of yoga became so popular that word spread to the West, and many westerners traveled to India to study with him. In 1966 Iyengar published *Light on Yoga*,

Yoga Controversy

Yoga is taught in many schools as part of physical education. Educators say yoga helps keep young people fit and helps them deal with stress. Some parents, however, are against the practice of yoga in schools. They believe that yoga's origin as a spiritual practice makes it an inappropriate subject for publicly funded schools. Although yoga is not a religion, its practice has been associated with Hinduism. In 2013, a group of parents in California brought a lawsuit against the Encinitas Union School District, saying the district's teaching of yoga violated their children's religious freedom. Encinitas school superintendent Timothy Baird admitted that yoga can be a spiritual practice, but that side of yoga was not being explored in the schools.

In July 2013, San Diego Superior Court Judge John Meyer ruled in favor of the school district and the yoga programs. Meyer said that the form of yoga being taught in the school district was strictly physical and did not include religious instruction. The parents have vowed to continue their fight and take the case to a higher court.

a manual of yoga asanas that became a worldwide best seller and greatly increased interest in yoga throughout the world. Students of Iyengar opened yoga studios all over the globe. To ensure that instructors adhered to his methods, Iyengar and his family established more than 180 Iyengar Yoga Institutes, where new yoga teachers are trained in Iyengar's method.

Another individual who helped popularize yoga in the West was Eugenie Peterson, a Russian actress who moved to India. She became a movie star in India, taking the stage name Indra Devi. After being diagnosed with a heart condition, she turned to yoga to improve her health. She became an expert in Krishna's flowing yoga style and traveled extensively, teaching yoga in China, India, Mexico, Russia, the United States, and Argentina. In 1947 she opened a yoga studio in Hollywood, California, that attracted many famous celebrities including Marilyn Monroe and Gloria Swanson. She also wrote a best-selling book titled *Forever Young, Forever Healthy*, which popularized the idea of yoga as a health and fitness regime and inspired women all over the world to take up yoga.

Types of Yoga

Many other yogis and yoginis opened studios in the West. As yoga spread, a wide variety of new styles of yoga were developed to suit Western culture. Most are offsprings of Hatha yoga and center on yoga as a fitness regime. Some are

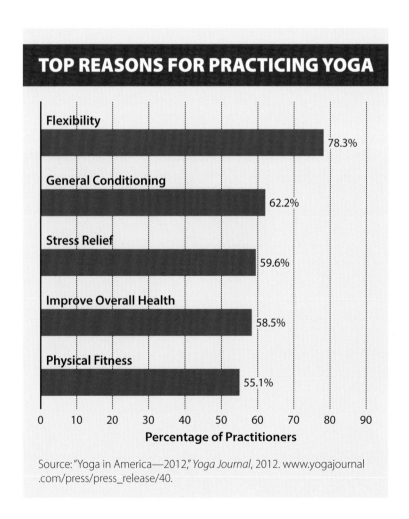

Source: "Yoga in America—2012," *Yoga Journal*, 2012. www.yogajournal.com/press/press_release/40.

geared to the general population, while other varieties focus on specific groups with special needs. As Krishna's son, yoga expert T.K.V. Desikachar, explains, "Yoga is not fixed. Yoga is creation. . . . We all have different experiences, different backgrounds, different perspectives on yoga and why it is important for us. So it is not surprising that different people find different things through . . . yoga teaching."[8]

There are more than one hundred styles of yoga. Power yoga is the most popular style of yoga in the United States. It is a physically demanding form of yoga geared toward athletic individuals. While practicing power yoga, individuals move rapidly through asanas synchronized with conscious breathing and little rest in between. Many of the postures resemble push-ups, sit-ups, squats, and other strength-training exercises.

Bikram yoga is even more rigorous. It is especially popular with men. It consists of two breathing exercises and a standardized series of twenty-six yoga postures that are performed for ninety minutes in a room that is heated to about 105 degrees F (40.5 degrees C). The room tempera-

Bikram is a rigorous form of yoga that consists of a standardized series of breathing exercises and postures performed for ninety minutes in a room that is heated to about 105 degrees.

ture is kept high so that the heat will help warm practitioners' muscles and loosen their joints, which promotes flexibility. It also helps exercisers to detoxify by sweating out impurities.

Other forms of yoga are gentler. Chair yoga, for example, is geared toward people with limited mobility. This form of yoga adapts traditional yoga postures so that they can be done while the practitioners sit in chairs, or stand using a chair for support. Chair yoga is particularly popular with elderly individuals. Prenatal yoga is another gentle form of yoga that is tailored to pregnant women. It concentrates on strengthening the pelvic and core muscles. Strong pelvic muscles help make delivering a baby easier, while strong core (abdominal and back muscles) helps pregnant women maintain good posture despite the pull of the fetus on the body. Prenatal yoga also focuses on yogic breathing that emphasizes exhaling. This is similar to the breathing exercises taught in natural childbirth or Lamaze classes, which help women relax during the birthing process. Once the baby is born, there is toddler yoga and kid yoga. In these forms of yoga, postures are adapted so that children can do them safely. Classes include games in which children imitate animals using yoga postures.

A Popular Practice

With so many varieties to choose from, almost anyone who is interested in practicing yoga can find a variety that suits his or her needs. Says Desikachar, "Anybody can practice yoga. But no one can practice every kind of yoga. It has to be the right yoga for the right person."[9] Currently, about 250 million people worldwide practice yoga. Of these, approximately 20 million are Americans. These individuals include celebrities, senior citizens, teenagers, adults, children, people with special needs, military personnel, and professional athletes. Yoga classes are offered in yoga studios, traditional fitness centers, healthcare facilities, and community and senior centers. Yoga retreats, cruises, and vacation packages are popular. Many school districts have added yoga to their physical education curriculum. In

A man and woman practice a modern form of yoga called Ashtanga in a suburban Atlanta, Georgia, park in 2012. Approximately 20 million Americans practice some form of yoga.

fact, yoga has become so popular that First Lady Michelle Obama made it a part of her Let's Move! national exercise program for children. Starting in 2009, yoga has been an annual part of the White House's Easter Egg Roll. The event has featured the Easter Bunny doing asanas and yoga classes for children on the White House lawn. Children attending, according to Broad, "took home a clear message about what the president and first lady considered to be a smart way of getting in shape."[10]

The practice of yoga has come a long way, transforming from a spiritual discipline practiced by Indian mystics to a health and fitness regime practiced by a wide variety of people all over the world.

CHAPTER 2

The Practice of Yoga

The modern practice of yoga involves performing specific postures coordinated with conscious breathing. The combination helps yoga practitioners focus their attention. Many yoga practitioners also practice yogic breathing exercises and meditation. They may apply the moral principles of traditional yoga to their daily life as well.

Warming Up and Cooling Down

Yoga is a form of physical exercise. As with all physical exercise, it is important to warm up and cool down before and after an exercise session. Warming up before working out prepares the body for more strenuous activity. It warms muscles by increasing blood flow to them. Warm muscles stretch more easily, making them less prone to injury. Warming up also helps yoga practitioners to start focusing their attention inward. Yoga warm-up exercises consist of two or three gentle yoga postures that are performed slowly with conscious breathing. Says yoga practitioner and blogger Suzanne Maguire:

> When you warm-up, you safely ease yourself, both physically and mentally, into the exercise. Warm-up postures . . . help you prepare for the activity ahead. You are improving your muscle flexibility, loosening

Students of a Sanskrit school in India perform the Savasana, *or corpse posture, during their daily yoga class.*

areas of your body, increasing blood flow to your extremities, and focusing your mind on the task ahead. A warm-up routine is just as important as the yoga practice itself."[11]

Similarly, yoga practitioners do cool-down exercises at the close of their workout. Suddenly stopping exercise causes muscles to stiffen, which makes them susceptible to injury. Cooling down serves to gradually end a workout. Cooling down after a yoga session involves slowly performing two or three gentle reclining yoga poses, followed by a period of relaxation in the form of *Savasana,* or the corpse pose. In the corpse pose, individuals lie completely still with their eyes closed, much like a corpse. They focus all their attention on their breathing, which helps them to turn off mental chatter and fully relax their bodies and minds.

Yoga Anatomy

Once individuals have warmed up, they can begin the physical practice of yoga. This entails stretching the body into different yoga poses, holding the pose through a specific number of breath cycles, and then moving the body into the next pose. Physiologists call this type of movement *static-active stretching*. It involves stretching a muscle or group of muscles as far as they can comfortably go, then holding the stretch without any assistance other than the strength of the muscles. An example is extending a leg up in the air and keeping it raised without any external support, such as a partner or bar. This type of stretching is difficult. Yogis and yoginis face the resistance of gravity and their own body weight. It takes flexibility, strength, and balance to get into and hold a pose. Because of the difficulty, yoga poses are usually held for only about ten to fifteen seconds each.

In order to understand the effect of static-active stretching on the body, it is helpful to understand how the musculoskeletal system works. The musculoskeletal system consists of the bones, joints, muscles, and connective tissues. The bones support the body and give it shape. The point where the bones connect to each other is called a *joint*. Joints work like hinges. They make the skeleton flexible. With the help of muscles, the joints make movement possible. Muscles attach to the bones by connective tissue. By pulling on a joint, muscles allow the body to move. As authors and yoga teachers Leslie Kaminoff and Amy Matthews explain:

> The muscles and bones work intimately together. . . . Without the structure and support of the skeletal system [bones], the muscles would be a puddle of contractile tissue with nothing to move. On the other hand, without the movement created by muscles, the bones would be unable to move through space and could only respond to forces outside the body travelling through them. Without connective tissue such as ligaments and tendons, bones and muscles would have no way to relate to each other.[12]

In order to generate movement, skeletal muscles work in pairs. For every movement, there is a muscle that contracts

A woman performs Natarajasana, *or Lord of the Dance pose, an example of static-active stretching in yoga.*

to move the joint and an opposing muscle that lengthens, which allows the bone to return to its original position. Contracting muscles are known as *agonists*, or prime movers, and stretching muscles are known as *antagonists*. Agonist and antagonist muscles are usually located on opposite sides of a joint, such as the biceps and triceps in the upper arms. Muscles can be both agonists and antagonists depending on the movement. In fact, they often switch roles. For instance, during a bicep curl, the biceps play the role of the agonist muscle and the triceps are the antagonist muscles. However, in a push-up the roles are re-

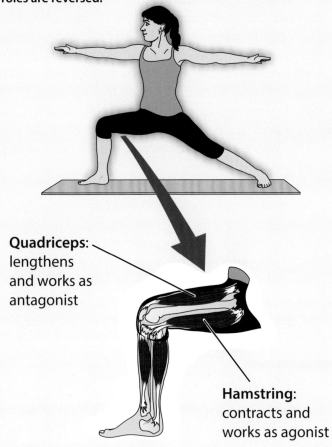

MUSCLE MOVEMENTS AND NEWTON'S THIRD LAW

In Warrior II pose, the hamstring contracts (action) and the quadriceps relaxes and lengthens (equal and opposite reaction), illustrating Newton's third law. When the leg is straightened to come out of the pose, the two muscles' roles are reversed.

Quadriceps: lengthens and works as antagonist

Hamstring: contracts and works as agonist

versed. Interestingly, the action of agonist and antagonist muscles illustrates Sir Isaac Newton's third law of motion, which states that for every action there is an equal or opposite reaction. Engineer, blogger, and yoga teacher Janet Tsai explains:

Yoga offers a particularly and deep understanding of action and reaction. . . . For example, when the hamstring [the muscle in the back of the upper leg] contracts, it bends the knee, pulling it towards the back of the body towards the hip. Its antagonist is the quadriceps [the muscle at the front of the upper leg]—when your quad engages, the knee joint extends and the leg is returned to straight. These muscle pairs exist all over the body—again, action and reaction.[13]

Other muscles known as *synergists*, or neutralizers, and *fixators*, or stabilizers, assist the agonist and antagonist muscles. Synergists assist the agonist muscles and minimize extra motion at the joint, while fixators help stabilize movement in other parts of the body. For example, in a bicep curl, the synergist muscle is the brachioradialis muscle, which is found in the forearm and helps move the elbow joint. The fixator is the rotator cuff muscle located at the shoulder joint.

Yoga practitioners seek harmony and balance between their minds and bodies and between the various muscles in the body. Just as the skeletal muscles work together, yoga postures are geared to working groups of muscles in concert with each other so that no muscle overpowers the others. "In yoga," says Tsai, "we are searching for balanced action, it's never only the quad or only the hamstring firing—it is always a blend of action and reaction simultaneously existing. In yoga, we practice fine tuning that blend of the two different muscle actions to enhance our stability and vitality."[14]

MEDITATE

3

Types of muscles in the body: cardiac (or heart), smooth (found in blood vessels, airways, and internal organs), and skeletal muscles.

The Postures

Yoga postures can be divided into five categories: standing, sitting, kneeling, prone, and inversion postures. Standing postures are the most frequently performed yoga postures. For example, in the Sun Salutation, a sequence of twelve postures, eight of the postures are standing poses. Authors and yoga teachers Georg Feuerstein and Larry Payne explain: "The standing postures are a kind of microcosm of the practice of asana as a whole . . . you can derive everything you need to master your physical practice from the standing postures. Standing postures help you strengthen your legs and ankles, open your hips and groin, and improve your sense of balance."[15]

Indian yoga expert and instructor Dinesh Dagar performs the Sirsasana yoga asana, an inversion posture that can counteract the effect of gravity on body.

Most yoga practice begins with the mountain pose, or *tadasana*—the basis for all standing postures. It involves standing straight and still with the feet pressed firmly to the ground and the arms hanging at the sides. Pressing the feet into the ground helps individuals to keep their legs straight. This is because gravity, the force that gives weight to objects and causes them to fall to the ground when dropped, pushes the body downward. This action, as per Newton's third law, causes a reaction in the form of the ground pushing back on the feet. The more firmly the feet are pressed, the stronger the upward push. Indeed, according to blogger and yoga teacher Kreg Weiss, "In the context of yoga, gravity provides the medium in which we can exert force, generate strength, and root against to form poses."[16]

Gravity also causes individuals to collapse or round their spines when they are standing or sitting, which is one reason many people have bad posture. Therefore, while in the mountain pose, yoga practitioners maintain awareness of their body position and symmetry. They make whatever adjustments are necessary to improve their alignment. Yoga practitioners maintain this body awareness in every pose. As lifelong yoga practitioner and actor Roger Lloyd-Pack explains: "Yoga has been a constant with me as a way of being in charge of my body particularly as I get older and understand how the body works. I love the wisdom of the standing poses. How if I have proper strong legs they will support my spine and my spine doesn't get tired. . . . I am able to be in charge of my body and not be a victim of what can happen to my posture if it is not cared for."[17]

From the mountain pose, depending on the type of yoga, individuals usually move into any one of a number of standing poses, many of which involve bending, lunging, or twisting, such as a forward bend, the warrior pose, or a reverse triangle pose. In a forward bend, practitioners start out standing upright with their arms raised over their heads. Then, they slowly fold their upper bodies downward bending from the hips until their palms touch the floor and their foreheads press against their shins. The force of gravity helps individuals to move into this pose and maintain it. The warrior pose is a lunging pose (back leg straight, front

Animal Postures

Many yoga postures are named after animals. Such postures imitate the way animals naturally move and stretch their bodies. For instance, in downward facing dog, yoga practitioners copy the way a dog stretches. To perform this posture, exercisers start on all fours, like a dog. Then they lift and straighten their knees. They keep their hands on the floor, their arms straight, and their heads between their arms as their hips rise. The cat posture also begins with yogis on all fours with their backs flat. Next, remaining on their hands and knees, they round their spines toward the ceiling and relax their neck and head, letting the head hang down toward the floor. This posture is often paired with the cow pose. To move from the cat to the cow pose, yogis move their back so that their stomach moves downward, their chest

Some yoga poses, such as downward facing dog, imitate the natural movements of animals.

moves up, and their head looks straight ahead, forming a table-like pose. Other animal-named yoga poses include cobra one, two, and three; the scorpion; the lion; the eagle; the turtle; and the camel.

leg bent at the knee). In all lunging poses the weight of the body relative to the force of gravity causes the front knee to bend. Gravity also helps yoga practitioners bend forward to reach their right hand to their left foot in the reverse triangle pose. At the same time, gravity provides resistance in this posture as the left arm is raised to the ceiling.

Twisting poses such as the reverse triangle require individuals to rotate their spine, hips, and shoulders and involve many muscle groups contracting or stretching. These include several groups of back muscles, neck muscles, and abdominal muscles. This type of rotation is based on the mechanical principles of *torsion* and *torsional loading*. Torsion is the twisting of an object by the exertion of force.

Torsional loading occurs when the force turns one end of the object in one direction, while the other end is motionless or twisted in the opposite direction. An example of torsional loading is using a screwdriver to loosen or tighten a screw. Tsai explains:

> We can feel this in our bodies simply by noticing what happens when we twist! Standing still in tadasana, or mountain pose, and twisting around the central axis of the spine creates a condition of torsional loading through the body. Since the feet are fixed in the earth, the resulting twisting action through the body is greatest at the greatest distance from the fixed point—the head! Twisting through the body is in this way an analog to torsional loading.[18]

Some seated postures also involve twists. Seated postures are performed on the floor and are a very basic part of yoga; in fact, the word asana literally means "seat." By doing seated postures, yogis and yoginis build their lower backs. This makes it easier to assume a seated cross-legged posture for long periods of meditation. In all cross-legged positions, individuals are working against the force of gravity, which can cause them to tip too far forward or backward. Keeping the spine straight helps prevent this from happening, as it strengthens and stretches the spine and back muscles. "The goal," according to Kaminoff and Matthews, "should be to find the position of the legs that allows the weight to fall most clearly from the spine through the pelvis into the sitz [buttock] bones and the support of the floor. . . . In this way, a minimum amount of muscular effort is needed to align the bones for support."[19]

Kneeling postures also stretch the lower spine. Some begin with the practitioner positioned on all fours, while other poses begin with individuals kneeling on the floor. Kneeling postures include twists, backbends, and relaxing poses. Some, such as the camel pose, which is essentially a kneeling backbend, or the child's pose, which

MEDITATE

The lotus position is a cross-legged, seated yoga pose associated with meditation. It is meant to resemble the beauty and symmetry of a lotus flower.

is a kneeling forward bend, take advantage of the force of gravity to facilitate and deepen the pose.

Backbends are also found in some supine, or reclining, postures, such as the cobra. Yoga practitioners believe that backbends are important because people bend forward frequently while doing things such as picking up items from the floor, pulling on pants, tying shoelaces, etc. Most people tend to bend from the waist rather than from the hip joints. Bending from the waist shortens or rounds the spine and can lead to spinal problems. Performing backbends stretches the chest, shoulders, and spine and counteracts problems caused by bending forward from the waist.

Inversion postures also strengthen the chest, shoulders, and back as well as the abdominal muscles and legs. Inversion postures such as headstands, shoulder stands, and handstands counteract the effect of gravity on body. Gravity causes the skin to droop and sag, the spine to compress, body fluids to be pulled toward the feet, and the heart to work hard to get blood to the brain. Inversion postures reverse the pull of gravity. During an inversion posture fresh blood flows to the head, and the spine stretches and straightens, which promotes better posture and a healthier back.

Breathing in Yoga Postures

Yoga practitioners synchronize their breathing, which is slow and deep, with yoga postures and movement. Yogis and yoginis move in one direction as they inhale and in the opposite direction as they exhale. Yoga practitioners also hold poses for a specific number of breaths. According to yoga teacher and alternative healer Ian Rawlinson:

> The basic principles of yogic breathing are very simple: Expanding movements are made on the inhalation. Contracting movements are made on the exhalation. Twisting movements are made on the exhalation. When you expand your body—e.g., raise your arms above your head—your chest naturally opens. When you inhale the chest and diaphragm also open. Thus, if you inhale with an opening movement of the body, movement and breathing are in harmony. Conversely,

Yoga practitioners say that practicing pranayama, *a breathing exercise, cleanses their bodies and calms their minds, preparing them for meditation.*

if you bend forward . . . your chest contracts. And when you exhale, the contraction of chest and diaphragm harmonizes movement and breathing. The same principle applies to twisting movements. When you are twisting into a posture, the thorax constricts, making it difficult to inhale. To maintain harmony between movement and breathing, it is necessary to exhale when twisting.[20]

The speed of each movement is also coordinated with the breath. Individuals begin consciously breathing as a movement begins and continue until the movement ends. This sounds easier than it is. It takes a lot of concentration to make sure that movement and breathing are in sync. Concentrating on breathing while doing yoga postures helps yoga practitioners to perform the postures more efficiently. It also forces them to focus all their attention on yoga practice, blocking out mental chatter and outside distractions. This type of deep concentration is essential to meditation practice and also has a calming effect on the mind.

Breathing Exercises

Some individuals practice specific yogic breathing exercises separate from movement, known as *pranayama*. Pranayama means "spreading the breath or life force," in Sanskrit. Pranayama practice encompasses a wide variety of breathing techniques. Exercises range from simple to complex. In

Yogic Chanting

A chant is a short, simple series of syllables or words that are sung or recited rhythmically. Some yoga practitioners participate in call-and-response group chanting sessions. These sessions, known as a kirtan, help individuals to focus their mind and relax. During a kirtan, a chant leader calls out words that group members chant back. Often a musician accompanies the chanting on small Indian drums known as tablas. Each chant usually lasts from ten minutes to a half-hour. The chants usually begin softly and slowly and gradually build in volume and rhythm. When a chant is finished, a period of silence follows. During this silent time, chanters meditate or simply relax their minds.

Chanting is a part of many religious practices and traditional rituals. Research has shown that chanting promotes a feeling of well-being and has a physiological effect on the body and mind. While chanting, a chanter's heart rate and blood pressure drop. Chanting also slows an individual's breathing rate from the normal twelve to fifteen breaths per minute to between five and eight breaths per minute.

every exercise, individuals practice breath control or conscious breathing, paying close attention to how they breathe and the rhythm of their breath. Usually, the goal is to slow and deepen breathing. While performing the simplest form of pranayama, yoga students consciously inhale and exhale deeply and smoothly through their nose, pausing for a few seconds between each inhalation and exhalation.

Yoga practitioners say that practicing pranayama cleanses their body and calms their mind, preparing them for meditation. To some extent, they are right. Science has shown that deep nasal breathing has a number of healthful effects. For example, breathing through the nose slows down breathing because nasal breathing entails breathing through the two small openings rather than a single large opening. Nasal inhalation filters out impurities such as pollen and dust in the air and warms the breath before it enters the lungs. Slow, deep inhalation also brings more oxygen into the lungs than shallow breathing. Therefore, more oxygen gets in the bloodstream and to the brain and vital organs, which helps them to work more efficiently. Conversely, deep, slow exhalations rid more impurities from the body than shallow exhalations. Moreover, deep, slow breathing stimulates the parasympathetic nervous system, lowering the heart rate and blood pressure, thereby calming the mind and body.

Meditation

Because pranayama helps individuals focus their attention inward and calms the mind, many yoga practitioners do breathing exercises as a prelude to meditation. As Desikachar explains, "When we follow the breath, the mind will be drawn into the activities of the breath. In this way pranayama prepares us for the stillness of meditation."[21]

Meditation entails freeing the mind of worrisome thoughts in order to relax the body, relieve stress, gain peace of mind, and/or spiritual growth. There are many different ways to meditate. In general, meditators use a concentration technique in which they focus their attention on one thing, such as their breath, an object, a sound, or an idea, until their minds are quiet and all stressful thoughts are gone. People who meditate report feeling extremely relaxed after as little as twenty minutes of meditation. A 2012 review of more than one hundred research studies on the effects of meditation found that meditation reduces stress, anxiety, and negative emotions and has a physiological effect as well. A number of studies using brain imaging technology have found that meditation causes an individual's brain waves to change. During meditation, brain waves shift from *beta waves* (rapid brain waves that dominate when the mind is moving from one thought to another) to *alpha waves* and *theta waves* (slower brain waves that occur when people are relaxed). Other studies have shown that meditation reduces blood pressure and the release of stress hormones.

A yoga group performs the Sukhasana *pose, a popular posture for meditation.*

Although the results of meditation are calming, learning to meditate can be frustrating. At first people may have trouble shutting off the chatter in their heads, or they may find that their minds wander. Some individuals repeat a mantra, either silently or audibly, to help them concentrate. A mantra is simply a word, sound, or phrase. The mantra *om* is commonly associated with yogic meditation. *Om* has no literal meaning. Ancient yogis believed that *om* was the first sound of creation. A mantra, no matter what it is, acts as an anchor for the mind. When people repeat a mantra their mind becomes engaged in the sound, which clears and calms the mind.

A Special Diet

In addition to performing asanas, pranayama, and meditation, some yogis and yoginis apply the moral principles of traditional yoga to their daily lives. These principles include doing no harm to yourself or other living creatures and keeping one's body clean. To fulfill these principles, some (but not all) yoga practitioners adopt an organic vegetarian diet. Vegetarians do not eat animal flesh. Some eat eggs and dairy products, and some, known as vegans, do not. By avoiding all forms of meat, yoga students keep from harming any animals that would be slaughtered for food. By choosing organic and whole, unprocessed foods (meaning foods that are raised and prepared without the use of pesticides, drugs, and other chemicals), they are protecting the environment and keeping harmful chemicals out of their bodies. "For yogis, food choices reflect personal ethics," says Blossom, a long-time yoga practitioner. "They are inextricable from our spiritual development."[22]

A vegetarian diet consists of vegetables, fruit, whole grains, seeds and nuts, beans, and in some cases dairy products and eggs. Although such a diet may seem limited, vegetarians can get all the nutrients they need. Nutrients are natural substances found in food that fuel and regenerate the body. Individuals need to get a balance of nutrients each day to be healthy. Nutrients are organized into six groups: proteins, fats, carbohydrates, vitamins, minerals, and water. Fruits and vegetables provide vegetarians with a rich supply of both vitamins and minerals. They get unsaturated fats, which are healthy fats that the body needs, in grains, nuts, seeds, and oils, and they get nutrient-dense complex carbohydrates in potatoes, beans, nuts, and whole grains. Getting enough protein, however, can be a problem. Proteins are composed of smaller components called amino acids. The body makes some amino acids, while other essential amino acids come from food. Foods that contain all the essential amino acids are called complete proteins. Most complete proteins are found in animal-based foods. There are a few non-animal-based foods that are complete proteins, too. These include soybeans, buckwheat, and quinoa. Other plant-based foods such as beans, nuts, seeds, and whole grains contain some, but not all, the essential amino acids and are therefore known as incomplete proteins. Vegetarians can ensure that they get all the protein they need by eating plant-based complete proteins or by combining incomplete proteins. For instance, combinations such as rice and beans, corn tortillas with beans, and peanut butter on whole grain bread provide complete proteins.

In addition, many individuals try to eat locally grown fruits and vegetables whenever possible. Locally grown foods typically contain more nutrients than those imported from other places. This is because the nutrient value of fruits and vegetables tends to decrease with time and there is a shorter time between the harvest and consumption of locally grown food compared to imported food. Moreover, purchasing locally grown food helps support the environment by helping to maintain local farm land and green space. "My choices are not only about serving myself but also serving the earth and the world in an authentic way,"[23] explains yogini Sianna Sherman.

The practice of yoga is complex. For some it is a physical fitness regime, for others it is a way to achieve peace of mind, or it may serve as a moral guide. Every facet of yoga has a particular purpose and effect on the body and mind. It is up to individuals to structure their yoga practice in whatever way meets their particular needs.

CHAPTER 3

Functional Fitness

Practicing yoga helps promote functional fitness. Functional fitness training prepares the body to perform real-life activities such as bending, lifting, running, stretching, and twisting safely and easily. Yoga helps improve balance, strength, range of motion, and flexibility, and it lessens stress—all of which are vital to functional fitness. As author Allison Kyle Leopold explains:

> What good is having the sexiest biceps in town if you can't scramble up subway steps with ease, run for a bus without knee pain or lift a toddler without wrenching your back? That's the premise behind . . . functional fitness. . . . Functional fitness means that the goal of working out is preparing your body so it can perform daily activities—walking, bending, lifting, climbing stairs—without pain, injury or discomfort.[24]

Even though practicing yoga can lessen an individual's chance of injury while performing everyday activities, like any form of exercise it can cause injuries. Taking certain safety precautions can help individuals limit their chance of injury.

A Special Form of Exercise

Yoga is unlike most Western forms of exercise in that it is not classified as *aerobic* or *anaerobic* exercise. Aerobic

exercise (also known as cardiorespiratory training) involves vigorous sustained physical activities that use oxygen to fuel muscle movement. It therefore elevates exercisers' need for oxygen, causing the heart rate and respiration rate to temporarily rise. The heart, which is a muscle, becomes stronger with aerobic exercise. Aerobic exercise also strengthens the lungs and improves the body's ability to use oxygen efficiently. Running, swimming laps, and biking are examples of aerobic exercise.

Anaerobic exercises are short-duration activities such as weight training. During anaerobic activity, the body uses up oxygen inside working muscles more quickly than it can be replenished. To fuel movement, the muscles use *glycogen* (stored carbohydrates) and other chemicals rather than oxygen. Anaerobic exercise builds muscle strength.

Although some forms of yoga such as power yoga and Bikram yoga are quite vigorous, in general yoga does

A yoga class performs the Warrior II pose. Many people practice yoga as part of their fitness regimen.

Yoga and Body Awareness

While performing yoga postures, yoga practitioners are encouraged to focus their attention inward, concentrating on their movements, body position, and the way the various muscles and joints involved in their movements feel. If a muscle feels too tense, or a position feels too awkward, they learn how to modify the movement to accommodate their bodies. This focus helps individuals develop muscle control. It also helps them become more tuned into their body both during yoga practice and in daily life. For instance, the general bodily awareness that yoga encourages makes yogis sensitive to the stretch and pull on their muscles and joints while they perform daily activities. Such awareness helps them to recognize when they are using their body in a dangerous manner, which lessens their chance of injury. It also helps them to recognize when they are unconsciously reacting to stress with their body by tensing their muscles, gritting their teeth, tightly clutching a steering wheel, or making a fist. It also teaches them how to release the tension through deep breathing and/or consciously loosening the muscles involved.

not raise the heart rate and respiration rate enough to be considered an aerobic activity. And, even though yoga builds muscle strength, it does not use glycogen to fuel movement and therefore is not considered an anaerobic activity. Yoga is a special form of exercise that is mentally and physically relaxing and trains multiple muscle groups to work together through stretching. Teaching muscles to work together is a key element of functional fitness. As athletic trainer Greg Roskopf, who has worked with athletes from the Denver Broncos, the Denver Nuggets, and the Utah Jazz, explains, "The key to functional exercise is integration. It's about teaching all the muscles to work together rather than isolating them to work independently."[25]

Yoga and Flexibility

One of the ways yoga practice helps enhance functional fitness is by increasing flexibility and range of motion. When some people think of yoga, they often envision incredibly flexible individuals stretching and twisting their bodies like rubber bands. Individuals do not have to be flexible to do yoga, but over time practicing yoga builds flexibility.

Flexibility describes the ability of the joints to move through a full range of motion. If a person has long, flexible muscles it helps in the flexibility of the joints. Range of motion describes the direction and distance a joint can be moved. Range of motion is measured in degrees by an instrument that measures angles. Although range of motion varies among people, medical professionals have established values for normal range of motion for each joint movement. For example, in the normal range of motion for rotation the spine falls between 20 and 45 degrees. As people age, their muscles tend to weaken, tighten, and shorten, decreasing their range of motion. "Our lives are restricted and sedentary," explains Thomas Green, a Lincoln, Nebraska, chiropractor, "so our bodies get lazy, muscles atrophy, and our joints settle into a limited range."[26] In addition, the water content of muscles and connective tissues (which lubricate the joints) naturally decreases as people age. This, too, lessens flexibility.

Limited flexibility and range of motion is linked to increased risk of pain and injury. Any rapid or awkward movement in which a person reaches, bends, or twists beyond their range of motion can cause muscles and tendons to tear or be damaged. This can happen in daily life or during athletic activities. It also can happen to individuals of all fitness levels who lack flexibility. "Even if you're aerobically fit, it helps to be limber, too, so your body can easily adapt to physical stressors,"[27] says Margot Miller, a physical therapist in Duluth, Minnesota, and a spokesperson for the American Physical Therapy Association.

MEDITATE

$10.3 Billion

Approximate amount Americans spend each year on yoga classes, apparel, supplies, and retreats.

Studies indicate that practicing yoga can progressively and permanently increase a person's flexibility. For example, a 2001 University of California, Davis, study tested the flexibility of ten sedentary college students before and after the subjects practiced yoga four times a week for eight weeks. After eight weeks, the subjects' flexibility increased

Eddie Solidon performs the one leg wheel pose at the Eastern Canadian Hatha Yoga Championship. Extreme flexibility can be achieved with yoga, but you do not have to be flexible to do yoga.

by nearly 200 percent. A 2005 University of Wisconsin study yielded similar results.

Performing asanas stimulates the production of fluids that lubricate the muscles, joints, and connective tissues. It also stretches and loosens tight muscles. Moreover, the effects appear to be long lasting. Physiologists believe that holding yoga postures for at least thirty seconds permanently lengthens muscle fibers. As a result, individuals are less prone to injury and can perform everyday movements with greater ease. Although this is important for everyone, older people especially benefit from increased flexibility. As people age, being more flexible can be a big factor in allowing individuals to maintain their independence. As blogger, yoga teacher, and physical therapist Shari Ser explains:

> I do yoga so I can do the other things in my life that are important to me. . . . It is the little things that we take for granted, like bending down to pick up a paper clip or tying our shoes. If I didn't have full mobility in my shoulders, hips, back, knees, or the dexterity to do a fine task like tying my shoes, I would either have to change my style of footwear or ask for assistance![28]

Flexibility is also vital to athletic performance, which is a part of many people's daily life. Many athletes cross train with yoga in an effort to increase their range of motion and flexibility. The role of range of motion in enhancing athletic performance can be explained by the physics formula: power output = range of motion × force. Basically, the formula states that the range of motion of a movement multiplied by the force applied to a movement equals the movement's power and speed. For instance, baseball players who have a full range of motion in the shoulders will produce a more powerful and faster swing than less flexible individuals. Yusef Boyd, an elite trainer with the National Academy of Sports Medicine explains:

> Proper flexibility is necessary for optimal performance. If a joint does not have normal range of motion due to overactive/tight muscles, performance will suffer. For example, if your calf muscles (gastrocnemius and soleus) are tight/overactive your ankle range of motion will be limited which means you cannot flex your foot

The Oakland
Athletics do early
morning yoga prior
to a spring training
workout. Flexibility
is vital to athletic
performance, so
many professional
athletes practice
yoga.

enough to get all your power on push off which would mean a slower race time, a missed rebound, a missed pass, inability to get to the net quick enough, and the list goes on. No matter the sport, proper flexibility is key if you want to perform at your absolute best.[29]

Strength and Endurance

Practicing yoga also helps increase muscle strength and endurance. Muscle strength is the amount of force a muscle or muscle group can produce against some form of resistance. Muscle endurance is the ability of a muscle or muscle group to repeatedly exert force against some form of resistance. Interestingly, having greater range of motion is important to muscle strength and endurance. This is because longer muscle fibers, associated with more flexible muscles, are stronger and can move faster than shorter muscle fibers.

In some respects doing yoga is similar to weight training, in that both activities work the muscles against some type of resistance. In weight training the resistance is a dumbbell, barbell, weight machine, or other piece of equipment. In yoga the resistance is the exerciser's own body weight. During yoga, individuals use their muscles to suspend and support themselves as they perform and hold yoga postures. This builds muscle strength and endurance. The University of California, Davis, study found that the subjects' muscle strength increased by 31 percent, and muscle endurance increased by 57 percent after only eight weeks of yoga practice. Increased strength and endurance makes performing and holding asanas easier. It also helps people perform everyday activities such as carrying a backpack full of books, lifting a toddler, or cleaning the house.

Yoga practice does not build large, bulging muscles. In yoga, muscle strength and flexibility are more important than muscle mass. In fact, the bulk of large muscles can interfere with flexibility and range of motion. Yoga balances muscle strength and flexibility. In contrast to weight training, which often concentrates on working muscles in isolation, yoga strengthens more muscles at a time than weight training. And it trains the muscles to work together, which is how muscles are used in daily life. As Jarrod Jordan, a New York City fitness trainer, explains:

> Your muscles may get stronger working on machines, but you're not creating synergy in the body. With seated bench press curls, while you're working your arms, the rest of your body remains inactive. By contrast, functional fitness workouts [such as yoga] challenge the body to work collectively as a whole, firing up the muscles in a sequential pattern.[30]

Fellow athletic trainer Greg Roskopf agrees:

> Most people can't even control their own body weight. They can't do a one-legged squat without falling over. They could lie down on a leg-press machine and press 500 pounds, but they don't have the muscular control for a one-legged squat because they don't have the stability or the muscles working together. . . . If you don't address integration, strong muscles get stronger and the weak ones stay weak."[31]

Yoga strengthens almost all the skeletal muscles, including the core muscles. These are the muscles that surround the spine, chest, and pelvis. Core muscles include the abdominal muscles, muscles in the mid and lower chest, back muscles, pelvic floor muscles, diaphragm muscles, and the muscles of the buttocks. The core muscles are very important to functional fitness because they stabilize the spine; transfer force between the limbs; align the spine, ribs, and pelvis to resist force, including gravity; and protect the spine from injury. All yoga postures build core strength. Certain poses such as the forearm plank and downward facing dog are especially strengthening to the core muscles.

Yoga and Balance

Having strong core muscles helps improve a person's sense of balance. Yoga practice, in general, improves balance and coordination. In terms of physical fitness, balance is the ability to maintain an upright position without falling and the ability to control body movement. Coordination is the ability to smoothly and efficiently move two or more body parts simultaneously, such as synchronizing the movement of the arms and legs.

Having good balance is a key component of functional fitness. It lessens a person's chances of tripping and falling. This is especially important considering the leading cause of hip fractures is falls. Falls are especially a problem for the elderly. Falls are the leading cause of fatal or serious injuries among people over eighty and the leading cause of admittance to nursing homes. Many elderly people limit their movements due to a fear of falling and the dangers a fall entails. Unfortunately, lack of movement causes a person's muscles to stiffen, which makes movement more difficult and significantly impacts quality of life. With this in mind, a 2012 University of Pennsylvania study looked at the effect of yoga practice on balance and fear of falling in a group of senior citizens with a mean age of eighty. The subjects, who were tested for balance and fear of falling pre- and post-

A yoga class in Seattle, Washington, practices a variation on the tree pose, which is used to improve balance.

study, participated in twice weekly one-hour chair yoga sessions for eight weeks. At the close of the study, most of the subjects showed better balance and reduced fear of falling, and three of the subjects were able to stop using assistive devices, such as walkers, altogether.

One way that yoga improves balance and coordination is by developing *proprioception*, which is the body's ability to sense its position and movement without a visual guide. By encouraging individuals to connect their body and mind, focusing on the here and now and on coordinating body movements, performing yoga makes individuals more aware of where they are spatially, and how their body parts work together. As Timothy McCall explains, "The regular practice of asana [with its focus on concentration on self and what you are doing with your body] steadily builds the ability to perceive what the body is doing."[32]

Although all yoga postures help with balance, some postures, such as the tree pose, which involves standing on one foot, emphasize balance. To do the tree pose, individuals stand with their right foot placed above their left knee and their arms raised straight over their head. Then they repeat the pose on the opposite leg. The posture requires keen focus and concentration. This emphasis on mindfulness not only improves balance but tends to calm the body and mind.

Yoga and Relaxation

Many people practice yoga as a way to counter stress. Modern life, with its myriad of psychological stressors and its emphasis on multitasking, can be nerve-wracking. Yoga helps individuals step out of the fast-paced world, quiet their minds, and relax. It does this in a number of ways. First, as with most forms of exercise, practicing yoga causes the brain to release endorphins and serotonin, chemicals that produce a feeling of general well-being. These feelings can last for up to two hours after yoga practice is over and are one reason people feel good after they exercise.

Other biochemical effects are more specific to yoga. Yogic deep breathing, slow flowing movement, and focus-

Yoga Apparel

Practicing yoga does not require any special kind of clothing. However, wearing certain garments and eschewing others makes yoga practice safer and more comfortable. For instance, yoga is traditionally done in bare feet. Bare skin provides better grip for performing yoga postures than socks. Plus, in many postures, individuals flex or arch their feet and spread or curl their toes. These actions are more easily done in bare feet than in shoes or socks.

Wearing comfortable, stretchy, form-fitting garments makes yoga practice easier and safer. Long, loose, bulky pants can get in the way, making it difficult for yogis to do certain poses, and causing safety hazards. Specially designed stretchable yoga pants are created with yoga practice in mind. They are form fitting without cutting into the waist as individuals bend and twist. They are also designed to end at or above the ankle, which prevents the possibility of tripping. Most yoga garments are made of a blend of cotton and Lycra. Cotton is a breathable fabric that absorbs perspiration, and Lycra is a synthetic material that is stretchable, comfortable, and maintains its shape.

ing on being present in the moment lessen stressful feelings by shifting the balance between the two branches of the autonomic nervous system. It turns off the sympathetic nervous system's "fight or flight" response and stimulates a relaxation response by the parasympathetic nervous system. As a result, the release of chemicals that help the body deal with a perceived threat is inhibited, and heart rate, respiration rate, and blood pressure decrease, making yoga practitioners feel calm and relaxed. As clinical psychologist Deborah Khoshaba explains: "Yoga practice changes the firing patterns of the nerves and chemical makeup of the body's fluids and blood gases that activates a relaxation response. By concentrating on carrying out the specific body posture and alignment of a pose and then holding it as you breathe deeply, the body starts to shift from a state of bio-chemical arousal and tension to calm and relaxation."[33]

The atmosphere that surrounds yoga practice adds to this calming effect. Many athletic activities are competitive. Trying to keep up with others is stressful. Yoga, on the other hand, is noncompetitive. Comparing yourself to others and/or judging yourself are discouraged. Instead, yoga practitioners are encouraged to turn their attention inward, listen to their body, and only do what their body can do. "Yoga provides attentional training and self-regulation," says Stephen Cope, director of the Institute for Extraordinary Living at Kripalu Center for Yoga and Health in Massachusetts. "In practicing yoga, we're training our awareness to attend to the flow of thoughts, feelings and sensations in the body—and to be with these different states without self-judgment."[34] This easy-does-it attitude helps makes yoga practice a peaceful activity and yoga class a safe and nurturing environment for people of all fitness levels.

The soft, slow music that is often played during yoga class adds to the tranquil atmosphere. Music has a strong effect on the emotions. Research has shown that listening to soft, gentle music lowers listeners' heart rate and respiration rate and accelerates the release of serotonin. Scientists do not know why this is so.

Ending yoga practice with the corpse pose also relaxes individuals. Yoga teachers typically guide students in relaxation exercises while they are in the corpse pose. This may involve instructing students to tune into their breath as they lay quietly, having them mentally relax their muscles one-by-one, and/or leading them in guided imagery, a practice in which students are guided to use mental images to picture themselves completely at peace. Some yoga teachers recite positive affirmations that encourage yoga practitioners to incorporate calmness and stillness into their daily lives. Many individuals find it helpful to recite the same affirmation when they are faced with a stressful situation. In fact, research has shown that saying a positive affirmation can reduce the release of stress chemicals, making it easier for individuals to cope with daily stressors.

Yoga Injuries

Despite all the ways in which yoga improves functional fitness, as with any type of physical activity injuries do occur. Overstretching is one common cause of injury while performing yoga. Overstretching can cause strains, sprains, joint dislocations, and torn or pulled muscles and tendons. Overstretching injuries are most likely to happen when

Instructors who are knowledgeable about exercise physiology can prevent yoga injuries.

people push themselves too hard rather than staying mindful and listening to their body. According to yoga teacher Glenn Black, "You have to set aside your ego and not become obsessive. . . . Asana is not a panacea or cure-all. In fact, if you do it with ego or obsession, you'll end up causing problems."[35]

Poorly trained yoga teachers who encourage students to overextend their bodies into unsafe positions or to assume a posture they are not ready for cause problems, too. Many yoga teachers are quite knowledgeable about exercise physiology, but some are not. Yoga teachers do not have to be licensed or certified, although many do attend yoga teacher training programs. It is important that yoga students find a qualified teacher before taking classes. Elizabeth Bennett injured her neck when a yoga teacher encouraged her to do a headstand despite her discomfort. As she explains, "When I hesitated, he called me a wimp. There are too many teachers who push unwitting students too far."[36]

Doing postures incorrectly or coming out of postures too quickly can also lead to injuries. For instance, wrist injuries often occur when individuals incorrectly put all their weight on their wrists when their hands are on the floor in positions such as downward facing dog. By spreading their hands wide, and pressing with their fingers, exercisers can better distribute their weight, thereby protecting their wrists from injury. Bending the knees slightly also lessens the pressure on the wrists. Lower back injuries, too, may occur when individuals round their backs in forward bending poses in which the spine should be kept straight.

MEDITATE

At the close of yoga class, instructors and students often bow to each other and say "Namaste," which means, "I bow to the divine spirit within you," in Hindi.

Attempting advanced postures before mastering simpler postures is also risky. Inexperienced yogis are more likely to do an advanced posture incorrectly, which can lead to injury. Judith Lasater, the president of the California Yoga Teachers Association and a physical therapist, says this occurs because "you may not have the necessary knowledge, flexibility, strength, and subtle awareness to proceed safely."[37] This is especially true for inversion

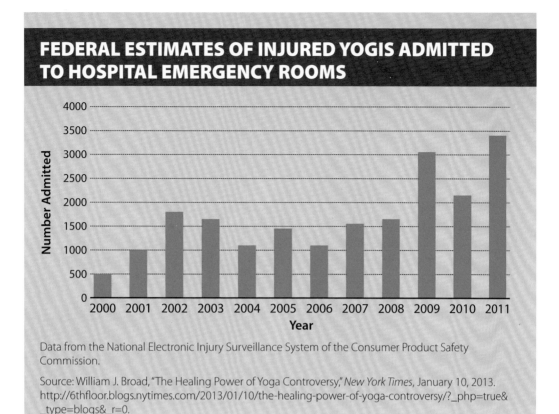

FEDERAL ESTIMATES OF INJURED YOGIS ADMITTED TO HOSPITAL EMERGENCY ROOMS

Data from the National Electronic Injury Surveillance System of the Consumer Product Safety Commission.

Source: William J. Broad, "The Healing Power of Yoga Controversy," *New York Times*, January 10, 2013. http://6thfloor.blogs.nytimes.com/2013/01/10/the-healing-power-of-yoga-controversy/?_php=true&_type=blogs&_r=0.

postures and poses involving backbends, which, when done incorrectly or too rapidly, can put extreme pressure on the neck and back and cause neck and spinal injuries. Even when done correctly, inversion postures can be dangerous. All inversion postures put the body in an unstable position, which poses a danger of falling over. In addition, going upside down increases pressure in the eyes, which can lead to torn retinas. Turning the head to the side during a shoulder stand can also strain muscles and ligaments in the neck or tear arteries in the back of the neck.

Equipment to Enhance Safety

Although practicing yoga does not require special equipment, certain products are designed to help individuals avoid injury. These include yoga mats, blocks, and straps.

Mats are essential for yoga and allow one to practice almost anywhere.

Yoga mats are probably the most popular yoga accessory. Yoga mats are designed to keep individuals' hands and feet from slipping during yoga practice. Mats also provide padding for joints and other parts of the body and cushioning in case of falls. Yoga mats are made from sticky material such as rubber or a type of vinyl known as PVC and usually have a slightly raised, bumpy texture. The texture adds friction against the floor's surface and the yoga practitioner's hands and feet, which improves traction and decreases chances of slipping. The more textured the mat, the more traction it provides. All mats are lightweight and portable and come in various sizes, colors, and thicknesses.

Yoga blocks also enhance stability and support for the body. The rectangular blocks are usually made of rigid foam or cork and come in different sizes. Yoga blocks work by simulating a higher floor. Practitioners place the blocks under their hands or feet to decrease the distance between their bodies and the ground. This makes it possible for individuals who are not flexible enough to perform a pose with proper bodily alignment to do so. The blocks help prevent overstretching, and they provide bodily support, which makes it easier to maintain balance in challenging poses. Because the blocks help with balance, they also make it easier for yogis and yoginis to hold poses longer.

Yoga straps, too, help yoga practitioners extend their reach. Yoga straps look like thick sashes or belts. They are usually made of cotton and have an adjustable plastic or metal buckle on one end. Generally, the straps are used to artificially lengthen the arms or legs so that yoga practitioners can perform and hold a pose with greater ease and proper alignment. For instance, the strap may be looped around the feet and grasped with the hands, which makes it easier to perform a seated forward bend without rounding the back, thereby lessening chances of injury.

Of course, using yoga props does not totally eliminate the possibility of injury. Yoga is, however, a gentle form of exercise that is less likely to cause injuries than more vigorous activities, and most yoga practitioners believe that the benefits of yoga far outweigh any risks. Yoga improves flexibility, range of motion, strength, endurance, and balance, and lessens feelings of stress—all factors that help make everyday living easier and more pleasant.

CHAPTER 4

Yoga and Physical Health

In addition to improving functional fitness, when yoga is combined with a healthy lifestyle it helps individuals maintain good health. The skeletal, immune, cardiovascular, and respiratory systems benefit from yoga practice. Yoga also helps relieve the symptoms of a number of health conditions. It is, therefore, frequently used therapeutically.

Yoga and the Immune System

Yoga practitioners often say that doing yoga keeps them healthy. They may very well be right. Research indicates that practicing yoga helps strengthen the immune system, thereby helping individuals to ward off disease. The immune system is the body's defense against infection. It consists of billions of specialized cells whose job is to attack and destroy harmful substances such as bacteria and viruses.

Many factors can weaken the immune system. One of the most significant is stress. When a person is under physical or psychological stress, a part of the brain known as the hypothalamus signals the adrenal glands, located above the kidneys, to release a cascade of hormones. Cortisol, which is also known as the stress hormone, is among these hormones. Cortisol is essential to helping the body overcome a crisis situation. In conjunction with other hormones, it increases blood pressure, heart rate, respiration rate, blood flow rate, and blood sugar. Cortisol also reduces body functions that are not essential for coping with a "fight or flight" situation. This includes inhibiting the release of *T cells*, white blood cells that are essential to the body's defense against viruses and bacteria.

Normally, the body's stress response is self-limiting. Once the perceived crisis is resolved, hormone levels return to normal. However, due to the myriad of stressors common to modern life, some people are persistently stressed, which causes their bodies to secrete excess cortisol. This is linked to an increased risk of developing infections, more severe infections, a recurrence of infections, delayed wound healing, and a less favorable response to vaccines by the immune system.

By shifting the balance from the sympathetic nervous system to the parasympathetic nervous system, thereby eliciting a relaxation response, yoga practice inhibits the release of cortisol. This allows the immune system to do its job more efficiently. A 2009 University of California, Los

A woman practices the Halasana, *or plow pose, a yoga position that helps maintain proper spinal cord alignment and overall health.*

Angeles, study that looked at the effect of yoga postures and meditation on the immune systems of patients with the human immune deficiency virus (HIV) found that subjects who practiced yoga had a significantly higher T cell count than the control group. Moreover, the more time the subjects devoted to yoga, the higher their T cell count. As researcher David Creswell explains, "What's really interesting is that we found a dose-response relationship between the amount of mindfulness meditation [including yoga] and T cell count. That is, the more people practiced, the better their T cells did. That indicates that the more you practice, if you do it on a weekly or daily basis, the better your outcome."[38]

Another study, conducted in 2013 at the University of Oslo, Norway, found genetic evidence of yoga's impact on the immune system. In this study, researchers examined genes circulating in the blood of ten subjects attending a week-long yoga retreat before and after they did yoga. The samples were compared to the blood samples of a control group that listened to music or went for walks while the other group practiced yoga. Based on previous research, the scientists knew that environmental, physical, and psychological factors can impact specific gene activity, which can alter a person's physiological state. The researchers found that two hours of yoga beneficially changed the activity of 111 genes that control immune cells. In comparison, walking or listening to music beneficially changed thirty-eight genes. As the researchers explain, "These data suggest that ... [the] effects of yoga practices have an integral physiological component at the molecular level, which is initiated immediately during practice, and may form the basis for the long-term stable effects."[39]

Yoga and the Respiratory System

Practicing yoga also appears to have a positive effect on the respiratory system. Poor posture, which is worsened by practices like hunching over a computer, compresses the chest. This causes muscles in the chest to shorten and tighten, which, in turn, lessens the ability of the chest and

Women at a yoga camp in India perform Anuloma Viloma Pranayama, *a breathing exercise believed to benefit both respiratory and cardiovascular health.*

ribcage to fully expand and contract during respiration. As a result, a person's depth and ease of breathing is compromised. Performing yoga postures counteracts this effect. Most yoga poses stretch and strengthen the shoulders, ribs, and chest muscles, thus making it easier for individuals to breathe deeply. To study the effect of yoga on breathing, a 2006 Thai study compared the respiratory functions of fifty-eight young, healthy subjects. Half participated in twenty-minute yoga sessions three times per week for six weeks and half acted as a control group. The researchers measured the subjects' breathing capacity at the start and end of the study. While the control group showed no change, the yoga group's breathing capacity improved. According to lead researcher Raoyrin Chanavirut, "This research suggests that short-term yoga exercise improves respiratory breathing capacity by increasing chest wall expansion and forced expiratory lung volumes [the amount of air a person exhales]."[40]

In addition to the biomechanical effect yoga practice has on the respiratory system, it improves breathing in another way. Doing asanas and breathing exercises makes individuals more aware of how they breathe and teaches them how to regulate their breath. As a result, they are more likely to breathe deeply. Ken, a yoga practitioner, explains: "There's a whole lot more to the way you breathe than simply something that's mechanical and keeps you alive. . . . I used to breathe very shallowly. I definitely breathe more deeply and more slowly now."[41]

Yoga and Cardiovascular Health

Yoga's respiratory benefits positively impact the cardiovascular system, which circulates blood through the body. It includes the heart, which acts as a central pump, and the blood vessels, which carry blood. The heart needs a large and constant supply of oxygenated blood to function properly. Individuals with optimal lung functions are better able to get more oxygen to their hearts than people with reduced lung functions. The more oxygen the heart receives, the more oxygen it can pump into the bloodstream to nourish all the cells in the body. Having more oxygen also allows the heart to pump less frequently and less forcefully. This decreases blood pressure, a measure of the pressure created as blood is pumped into the arteries. In fact, research has found an inverse relationship between lung function and blood pressure. This means the more efficient a person's respiratory functions, the lower their blood pressure, and vice versa. This is important because, over time, high blood pressure can damage or weaken the heart.

Yoga's ability to elicit a relaxation response also beneficially affects blood pressure. When the body is under stress, arteries constrict and the heart pumps faster and harder, which causes blood pressure to rise. Yoga's ability to neutralize the sympathetic nervous system and relax the body causes the arteries to expand, the heart rate to slow, and blood pressure to drop. Moreover, regular yoga practice appears to keep blood pressure levels down.

MEDITATE

By stimulating blood flow, stretching the spine, and getting more oxygen to every cell in the body, yoga helps to fight fatigue and make people feel more energetic.

Yoga for Everyone

Yoga practice offers wheelchair-bound people the same benefits as it does ambulatory people. Michael Sanford, a yoga teacher who became paralyzed as a teenager, is a pioneer in the field of adapting yoga for the differently abled. In a 2013 interview, he talks about his work:

> Our bodies stay healthier when they move. . . . So how do you live in your body fully if you're not able to exercise and move in the same way as everyone else? The principles of yoga do not discriminate. In our approach to working with someone in a wheelchair, we think about what's universal to every pose, regardless of how complicated it is. Rather than specific poses, we focus on the sensations—the sensation of feeling grounded, sensation of feeling balanced, sensation of expansion and sensation of rhythm. . . . The way you get access to yoga if you live with a physical limitation is to start exploring what's universal to each yoga pose and recreating that in your own experience. Another practical step in adapting yoga is breaking down parts of the pose, and thereby getting a sense of the whole.

Quoted in Laura McMullen. "Yoga for People in Wheelchairs." *U.S. News & World Report*, April 19, 2013. http://health.usnews.com/health-news/health-wellness /articles/2013/04/19/yoga-for-people-in-wheelchairs.

Yoga's effect on stress benefits cardiovascular health in yet another way. Research links high stress with excess cholesterol levels. Cholesterol is a soft, waxy fat produced by the liver and found in certain foods. It is carried by proteins known as lipoproteins in the bloodstream. The body uses cholesterol to build cell walls. Too much cholesterol, however, can clog coronary arteries, blocking the flow of blood and leading to heart disease.

A number of Indian studies indicate that regular yoga practice reduces blood cholesterol as much as thirty points. There is no definitive reason why, but scientists believe it is due to yoga's ability to activate the parasympathetic nervous system. In an article on the American Heart Association's website, M. Mala Cunningham, a counseling psychologist and mind-body health expert, explains: "Hand in hand with leading a heart-healthy lifestyle, it really is possible for a yoga-based model to help prevent . . . heart disease. . . . After 12 weeks [of yoga practice], you may see a dramatic increase in exercise functionality, and blood pressure and cholesterol levels may decrease."[42]

Strong Bones

The Warrior II pose can help build bone strength by putting more pressure on the humerus bone.

Yoga also helps strengthen bones. The human body constantly removes old bone cells and forms new ones. From childhood through early adulthood, bone formation usually surpasses the removal of old bone. However, as people age, bone formation tends to slow down. This is especially true for older women, who can lose up to 20 percent of their bone mass after menopause due to changes in their body chemistry. Losing bone mass is a problem because thin bones are weaker and more likely to fracture. All weight-bearing exercises strengthen bones and reduce bone loss. This includes performing standing yoga postures. In fact, because

of the positioning of lunging yoga poses such as Warrior II, where the front knee is bent and the arms are raised parallel to the shoulders, doing yoga actually causes the bones to bear extra weight. That makes this type of exercise more beneficial for building bone strength than weight-bearing exercises such as walking or running. "By bending the front knee to 90 degrees, you do more than simply bear weight in the front leg; you magnify the force on the femur [thigh] bone," explains Loren Fishman, an assistant clinical professor at the Columbia College of Physicians and Surgeons in New York, New York. "Because you're holding your arms out away from your body, you're putting a lot more stress on the head of your *humerus* [a long bone in the upper arm] than you would if they were hanging at your sides."[43]

To examine the effects of yoga on bone density, Fishman led a 2009 study in which he enrolled eighteen elderly subjects, eleven of whom performed ten minutes of standing yoga postures every day for two years, and eight of whom acted as a control. Fishman measured the subjects' bone density at the start and close of the study. Not surprisingly, the control group either lost or maintained their original bone density, while 85 percent of the yoga group gained bone mass.

A Counterpart to Traditional Medicine

In addition to benefitting healthy individuals, yoga helps to relieve the symptoms of a number of health conditions. Using yoga as a form of medical treatment is known as yoga therapy. Yoga therapy is a type of alternative medical treatment. Alternative treatments are treatments that are not widely accepted by the traditional medical community in the United States. Unlike traditional medical treatments, most alternative treatments have not undergone conclusive studies to prove their safety and effectiveness. Also, there are no universal standards for alternative therapists. Therefore, their training, education, and experience vary widely.

Many yoga therapists complete respected training programs, but some do not. In order to find a qualified therapist, patients can get referrals from disease advocacy groups,

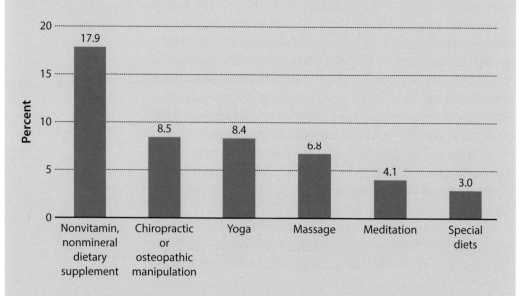

YOGA AMONG THE MOST USED COMPLEMENTARY MEDICINE APPROACHES

Percentage of adults in the United States who used selected complementary health approaches in 2012.

Data from Centers for Disease Control and Prevention/National Center for Health Statistics (CDC/NCHS) National Health Interview Survey, 2012.

Source: Jennifer A. Peregoy et al., "Regional Variation in Use of Complementary Health Approaches by U.S. Adults," NCHS Data Brief, no. 146, April 2014. http://www.cdc.gov/nchs/data/databriefs/db146.pdf.

traditional healthcare professionals, yoga therapist training programs, or organizations such as the Yoga Alliance. Working with a qualified therapist helps individuals avoid possible problems, as does combining yoga therapy with traditional medical treatment in a method known as complementary therapy. This method allows patients to reap the benefits of both yoga therapy and traditional medical treatment. In fact, some medical schools are offering courses on integrating yoga therapy into mainstream medicine, and more and more medical professionals are recommending it as an adjunct treatment. Harminder Kauer, a Clarksburg, Maryland, physician, is one of these professionals. She explains: "It takes one case to be successfully treated, then your mind is open to it."[44]

Like the practice of yoga, which is a holistic discipline that links the mind and body, yoga therapy takes a holistic approach to health issues. While traditional medical interventions focus solely on the chief complaint, holistic therapy focuses on the whole person and how various physiological and psychological factors may impact the primary complaint. For example, conventional medical treatment for knee pain is likely to involve pain medication, physical therapy concentrating on the knee, and/or knee surgery. In comparison, because the movement of one joint affects nearby joints, yoga therapy for knee pain is likely to consist of exercises that stretch and strengthen the knees, hips, thighs, ankles, and feet. It might also include exercises to improve body alignment and posture, breath work, meditation, relaxation sessions to help patients deal with pain and psychological stress, and dietary changes aimed at improving general health. As Janice Gates, president of the International Association of Yoga Therapists explains, "Yoga therapy is very much about the whole person. It is

A yoga therapist works with a patient at the Cleveland Clinic Center for Integrative Medicine, which has been in operation in Ohio since 2006.

complementary to physical therapy, but we take into account that . . . pain may be related to an emotional element, or it may be from lifestyle, some pattern that is not serving them, physical movement patterns or other patterns."[45]

Yoga therapy is offered in 93 percent of integrative medical centers (medical centers that combine traditional and alternative medical treatments), as well as in a growing number of conventional medical clinics, physical therapy centers, and yoga studios. Sessions are typically one-on-one or small groups of two to four people. Upon a patient's first visit, along with getting information about the patient's primary problem, the yoga therapist evaluates the patient's body symmetry and alignment, posture, muscle tone, strength, flexibility, age, health history, lifestyle choices, and general emotional state. Then the therapist develops a

Becoming a Yoga Teacher

There are many paths a person can take to become a yoga teacher. Some yoga studios employ experienced yoga practitioners with no formal training as instructors. However, most require instructors to have completed a minimum of two hundred hours of yoga teacher training. Some require five hundred hours of training.

Many yoga studios offer training courses for potential teachers, as do yoga retreats. Training schedules vary. Some programs are intensive, with classes meeting each day for a month or two. Other programs meet only a few evenings each week and may last about one year. Tuition can cost at least $3,000.

The Yoga Alliance, a nationally recognized organization, registers yoga teacher training programs that meet certain standards and offers potential yoga teachers referrals to registered yoga instruction programs. Individuals who complete a teacher training program registered by the Yoga Alliance may use the abbreviation RYT (Registered Yoga Teacher) after their name.

customized therapy program for the patient. The program is likely to consist of various yoga postures and practices that have been modified to address each case. "We recognize that not every pose is for everybody," said Robin Rothenberg, a Seattle yoga therapist. "If you are a 20-something dancer, that is one thing and if you are a 50-year-old computer programmer, that's a different thing."[46]

During each session, the therapist works with the patient. As the patient's health needs change, the therapist modifies the treatment plan to suit the individual's changing abilities. According to McCall, "The approach tends to be hands-on, tailored to the individual based on needs, abilities, and responses as well as the teacher's or therapist's observations and any contraindications. Props such as blankets, bolsters, and straps may be employed to make postures more comfortable and safer, or postures themselves may be modified."[47]

Yoga and Back Pain

Individuals turn to yoga therapy for a variety of conditions. One of the most popular uses of yoga therapy is to help relieve the symptoms of chronic back pain. That is back pain that lasts at least three months. Chronic back pain is caused by degenerative conditions such as arthritis or bone disease, a ruptured spinal disk, strained ligaments, nerve damage, aging, normal wear and tear on the spine, obesity, poor posture, stress, a sedentary lifestyle, or the formation of scar tissue (which lacks the strength or flexibility of normal tissue) after injuries, among other reasons. Sometimes, the exact cause is difficult to determine. Finding relief for chronic back pain can be difficult. Traditional treatments, such as pain relief medication or surgery, can be risky. Moreover, these treatments, as well as physical therapy, rarely treat other factors such as stress or bad posture that aggravate the problem, or may even be the cause of the problem. Yoga therapy, on the other hand, seeks to identify and treat every factor that may be involved. This includes stress, which can cause back muscles to tighten and spasm in reaction to the "fight or flight" response; poor posture, which puts strain on the spinal disks; muscle weakness or tightness; problems with groups of muscles not working together properly; and lack of body awareness. Yoga has been proven to effectively address all of these issues. For example, yoga postures stretch, strengthen, and loosen groups of muscles. As a result, yoga exercises for back pain involve not only back muscles but also connecting muscles including those in the hamstrings, abdomen, and neck, which are often part of the problem. As author Julie Gudmestadt explains:

Men and women with lower back pain participate in a special yoga class at the Boston Medical Center in 2011.

> Tight hamstrings affect posture and the health of the lower back by exerting a constant pull on the sitting bones, tipping the pelvis posteriorly and flattening the normal curve of the lumbar spine. Overly strong or tight abdominal muscles may also contribute to a habitually flattened lower back. Tight abdominal muscles pull up on the pubic bones, again contributing to posterior tilt, especially if combined with tight hamstrings. They also pull down on the front rib cage, contributing

to forward-slumped posture. This posture, with posterior-tipped pelvis and forward-slumped trunk, puts chronic strain not only on the discs, but also on the lower back muscles.[48]

Yoga therapy also develops body awareness, which makes people more conscious of bad postural habits and the way they use their bodies to perform everyday activities that can worsen back pain. In addition, performing yoga postures reduces stress, as do breathing exercises and meditation. Reducing stress stimulates the release of *dopamine*, a hormone that promotes a feeling of well-being, and relaxes the muscles, which relieves pain. Indeed, a 2013 German study that reviewed the outcomes of 967 patients who received yoga therapy for chronic back pain found that yoga therapy was very effective in providing pain relief.

Yoga and Cancer

Yoga therapy also is often used as a complementary treatment for cancer. Specially modified gentle asana practice, deep breathing, guided imagery, and meditation appear to be helpful in lessening the stress, pain, and fatigue that are symptomatic of cancer and of cancer treatments such as chemotherapy, surgery, and radiation.

Yoga as a complementary treatment for cancer is so promising that several well-known cancer treatment centers offer restorative yoga therapy classes as part of their treatment program. Among these institutions are California's Stanford Cancer Center, New York's Memorial Sloan-Kettering Cancer Center, and Texas's MD Anderson Cancer Center. In fact, the National Cancer Institute has given the MD Anderson Cancer Center a $4.5 million grant to conduct ongoing research on yoga's effect on cancer patients. Preliminary findings validate the usefulness of yoga therapy. In one study, 191 women undergoing radiation treatment for breast cancer were randomly divided into three groups: a group that did yoga three times a week for the six weeks of radiation treatment, a group that did simple stretches in the same time frame, and a control group. Throughout the six weeks, and for six months after the study ended, the

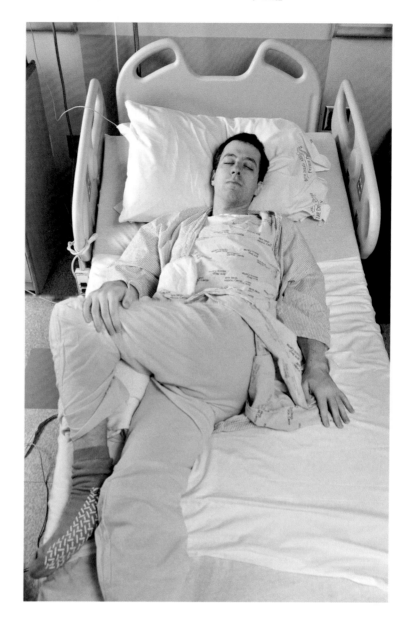

A leukemia patient practices a yoga routine in his bed at Beth Israel Hospital in New York City. Yoga can lessen the stress, pain, and fatigue that accompany cancer and cancer treatment.

subjects' cortisol levels were monitored. The yoga group had the greatest decline in cortisol levels. Keeping cortisol levels down during cancer treatment is important because high levels of cortisol negatively impact the immune system. Reducing the chemical helps cancer patients lessen their risk of contracting an infection. For cancer patients, having an infection often means that potentially life-saving treatments such as surgery, chemotherapy, or radiation must be cancelled or delayed.

Cancer treatments are quite demanding. Yoga appears to help individuals get through these treatments more easily. Doing yoga increases blood flow and the delivery of oxygen to tired cells, which enhances the body's ability to clear out toxins that build up during cancer treatment. In many cases, this helps reduce debilitating side effects. This is important because when side effects are too great, treatment may need to be stopped or reduced. Yoga also helps restore flexibility and range of motion for individuals recovering from cancer surgery. "During treatment," explains Stephanie Cornelius, who was diagnosed with cancer in 2010, "yoga was the only thing that made me feel better. Yoga relieved the side effects of chemo. Because of yoga, I had full range of motion."[49]

In addition, the effects of yoga therapy appear to be long-lasting. As part of the MD Anderson study, the subjects answered questions about their level of fatigue, sleep quality, physical functioning, overall physical and emotional health, stress level, and quality of life during radiation treatment and for six months thereafter. Both the stretching and yoga groups reported decreased levels of fatigue. But only the yoga group reported improved emotional and physical health, sleep quality, and physical functioning in the six months following radiation treatment. These benefits are significant because between 70 to 96 percent of recently treated cancer patients complain of fatigue, and 30 to 50 percent complain of poor quality sleep. Experts believe the reasons for these problems are physical and psychological. According to researcher Lorenzo Cohen, "Combining mind and body practices that are part of yoga clearly have tremendous potential to help patients manage the psychosocial and physical difficulties associated with treatment and life after cancer. . . .

MEDITATE

2 hours

Recommended amount of time to wait after a meal before beginning yoga practice. Eating a meal before exercising can make individuals feel unenergetic and can cause discomfort.

Teaching patients a mind-body technique like yoga as a coping skill can make the transition less difficult."[50]

Yoga therapy for cancer has another beneficial effect. Participating in small group sessions gives individuals with cancer and/or those recovering from the disease a safe, nurturing place where they can temporarily escape from the challenges they face and connect with other individuals who share their struggles. Also, by allowing individuals to participate in their treatment, yoga therapy sessions empower cancer patients and make them feel more in control. As Amanda Nixon, a breast cancer survivor, explains:

> At the age of 27, I was diagnosed with an extremely rare, aggressive form of breast cancer. . . . Immediately following my diagnosis, my life became a whirlwind of chemotherapy, radiation treatments, a mastectomy and reconstructive surgeries. . . . It wasn't until I stepped foot into my first Cancer Therapy Yoga class that something clicked. Here I was able to reconnect with my body and focus my mind, surrounded by other beautiful breast cancer survivors. The class was fun, restorative, and gentle enough for beginners. I was in a safe place where I felt accepted, supported, and loved. From then on, I was hooked. . . . Yoga has helped me manage stress, improve my sleep and digestion, increase my range of motion, reduce pain, and most importantly, stay healthy (aka help avoid a recurrence of breast cancer).[51]

Yoga therapy has also been found to be useful in treating the symptoms of many other health conditions including multiple sclerosis, Parkinson's disease, headaches, HIV/AIDS, and diabetes. Although yoga is not a miracle cure-all, a growing body of research indicates that it can help ill individuals feel better and healthy individuals maintain good health.

CHAPTER 5

Yoga and the Mind

In addition to enhancing physical health and functional fitness, practicing yoga has a number of beneficial effects on the mind. Research indicates that yoga positively affects mood, emotions, alertness, memory, sleep, self-control, and the very structure of the brain.

Yoga and Mood

A mood is an emotional state that usually lasts for hours or days. Moods are typically positive or negative, as in a good or a bad mood. Moods tend to influence the way individuals react to and perceive people and events. Psychiatric illnesses such as depression and bipolar disease, which affect mood and interfere with an individual's daily life, are mood disorders. Research indicates that practicing yoga can lift a person's mood and help people suffering from mood disorders. Amy Weintraub, a pioneer in the field of yoga and mental health and a victim of depression, found relief from her illness through yoga. "I had a history of depression. . . . I started practicing yoga for depression daily, and after about nine weeks I started to notice a real significant difference in my mood—I was more balanced and elevated,"[52] she explains.

Yoga affects mood on many levels. Scientists already know that feelings, emotions, and moods are influenced by

Yoga enthusiasts participate in the 2012 Mind Over Madness summer solstice event in Times Square in New York City. The frenetic location is meant to highlight yoga's calming psychological effects.

chemical changes in the brain. It is also known that many mental disorders are associated with an imbalance of brain chemicals known as *neurotransmitters*, which are substances that allow brain cells or neurons to communicate with each other. There are billions of neurons in the brain. They communicate with each other across tiny spaces known as *synapses*. Communication between neurons is a chemical process. When a neuron is stimulated, it releases a neurotransmitter. The neurotransmitter travels across the synapse to the receiving end or receptor of the next neuron. Other neurotransmitters on the receptor produce a signal that either sends the message on or stops the message from moving forward. Different neurotransmitters serve different purposes. One neurotransmitter in particular, *gamma-aminobutyric acid* (GABA), has been linked to positive mood and emotion. GABA's main job is to slow down brain and nerve cell activity. It works by keeping neurotransmitters that are carrying stress-related messages from moving forward. This helps derail a stress reaction and promotes relaxation. "GABA," explains author and psychiatrist Emily

Deans, "is the chief inhibitory neurotransmitter in the . . . nervous system. It cools things off and chills things out. People with depression and anxiety have been shown to have low amounts of GABA."[53] On the other hand, high levels of GABA are linked to feeling relaxed and happy.

With this in mind, researchers at Boston University conducted two studies in 2007 and 2010 examining what, if any, biochemical effect yoga has on GABA levels. In the first study, the researchers used brain imaging to measure GABA levels in the brains of eight subjects who had been practicing yoga at least twice a week for a minimum of two

Yoga Manners

In the book *Yoga for Dummies*, authors Georg Feuerstein and Larry Payne offer the following tips on proper yoga class etiquette:

- Show up on time; don't wander into class "fashionably" late. It's rude and disturbing to others.
- Leave your shoes, chewing gum, cellphones, pagers, and crummy attitudes outside the classroom.
- Bathe and take a restroom break before your yoga session.
- Keep classroom conversation to a minimum—some people arrive early to meditate or to just sit quietly.
- Be sure to take your socks off if you practice on a slippery surface.
- Avoid excessive, clanky jewelry.
- Do not wear heavy perfume or cologne.
- Sit near the door or window if you require a lot of air.
- Sit close to the instructor if you have hearing difficulties; many teachers speak softly to generate the right mood.
- If you have used any props in class, put them away neatly.

Georg Feuerstein and Larry Payne. *Yoga for Dummies*. Hoboken, NJ: Wiley, 2010.

years. The subjects' GABA levels were measured before and after they participated in an hour-long yoga session. The results were compared to those of a control group. After the yoga session, the subjects' GABA levels increased an average of 27 percent. The control group showed no change. The researchers also found that the subjects who practiced yoga over the longest period of time, and those who practiced yoga more than twice weekly, had the greatest increase in GABA. The second study yielded similar results.

Another study conducted at the University of Wisconsin in 2011, took a different approach. In this study, researchers used brain imagery to look at the brain activity of yoga practitioners. Subjects in this study practiced Hatha yoga and meditation for nine half-hour sessions over the course of five weeks. Researchers compared the subjects' brain activity at the start and end of the study. They found that the yoga and meditation practice caused neural activity in the subjects' brains to shift from the right part of the prefrontal cortex (the front part of the brain) to the left part. Activity in the left part of the prefrontal cortex is associated with happiness, positive moods, and a feeling of well-being. Once again the subjects who were the most experienced yoga practitioners showed the biggest change. "Suggesting," according to Timothy McCall, "that with sustained practice you can shift your emotional baseline towards greater levels of happiness."[54]

Reducing Anxiety

In addition to elevating happy feelings, yoga helps relieve anxiety. According to the American Psychological Association, "Anxiety is an emotion characterized by feelings of tension, worried thoughts and physical changes like increased blood pressure."[55] Yoga reduces anxiety biochemically by raising GABA levels and decreasing cortisol levels. In fact, GABA has such a strong effect on lessening anxiety that most antianxiety medications work by stimulating the release of GABA. Conversely, high levels of cortisol are known to increase nervousness and feelings of anxiety. Therefore, it is not surprising that yoga, with its ability to

Yoga postures stretch tense muscles and reduce the nervous energy associated with anxiety.

reduce cortisol secretion and increase GABA production, lessens anxiety.

Yoga helps ease anxiety psychologically, too. By teaching individuals to detach from their thoughts and focus their attention inward, yoga helps individuals become more aware of their thought patterns. As a result, yoga practitioners are better able to recognize when their thoughts are becoming anxious. They can then employ yogic tools to shift their thoughts and lessen their anxiety. This can be done through asana practice, which stretches tense muscles and reduces nervous energy associated with anxiety; reciting a calming affirmation; meditation; or by using yogic breathing to calm their body and mind. As Mesa, Arizona, counselor and therapist Art Matthews explains:

> The reason yoga can be very helpful for people with anxiety . . . is that it involves breathing techniques, muscle stretching, physical activity and the mental activity of shifting and maintaining focus on the present moment and away from thoughts that are perhaps distorted and cause distressing feelings. . . . Doing this requires that we set aside the other thoughts and judgments running through our minds about who did what to whom, how I can get everything done, what others think of us, the injustices of life, etc. Yoga doesn't change any of those things but helps us to build resilience and tolerate things in our lives.[56]

Yoga and Post-Traumatic Stress

In addition to helping reduce ordinary feelings of anxiety, yoga has been shown to relieve the symptoms of post-traumatic stress disorder (PTSD), a type of anxiety disorder that affects some, but not all, people who have experienced a traumatic event. Although it is common for people to have emotional issues after experiencing a traumatic event, these issues normally decrease over time. This is not the case for people with PTSD, who keep reliving the event in their minds. They often have sleep disturbances, become easily agitated or angered, have an exaggerated response to certain sounds or sights, have difficulty concentrating, have a disrupted sense of time, and feel disconnected from their own body and mind and their surroundings.

Physiologically, researchers believe PTSD occurs due to a malfunction in the autonomic nervous system. It appears that trauma can cause

MEDITATE

Slow, deep yogic breathing can raise carbon dioxide levels in a person's body. Carbon dioxide acts as a natural sedative and helps people sleep.

Yoga in Prisons

The Prison Yoga Project offers yoga classes to men and women in prisons. The project is based on the theory that learning how to do yoga gives prisoners a tool for handling stress and anger, and it helps them to better understand themselves. As a result, they can handle life in prison better and should be less likely to become repeat offenders upon their release. According to an article on the Give Back Yoga (a charitable organization that helps fund the Prison Yoga Project) website:

> Yoga can help prisoners to change trauma-induced, unconscious behavioral patterns like impulse control issues, mood disorders, violence, addiction and PTSD—usually, the behaviors that landed them in jail in the first place. This shift can help to get them out of the prison system where they are a financial burden on society and into their communities where they themselves can give back.

Studies that have investigated the effect of yoga practice on prisoners found that participants report feeling less stressed, anxious, hostile, and depressed. They also report having improved self-esteem. They also are less likely to be reincarcerated than their peers.

"Prison Yoga Project." Give Back Yoga. http://giveback yoga.org/projects/prison-yoga.

Prisoners participate in a yoga class at the Luther Luckett Correctional Complex in LaGrange, Kentucky.

a breakdown of the parasympathetic nervous system. This breakdown immobilizes the parasympathetic nervous system, while keeping the sympathetic nervous system on constantly.

PTSD can affect anyone who has experienced a trauma, but it is especially common in war veterans. According to the Veterans Administration, approximately 20 percent of Iraq and Afghanistan war veterans have PTSD. Since yoga is known to stimulate the parasympathetic nervous system, the military has been investigating if yoga can help ease PTSD symptoms. In a study at Walter Reed Army Medical Center in Washington, D.C., after practicing yoga for twelve weeks, nine soldiers with PTSD reported sleeping better and feeling more in control of their lives. A similar 2010 study at Harvard Medical School found that veterans with PTSD showed marked improvement in their symptoms after ten weeks of yoga. Lead Harvard researcher Bir S. Khalsa explains:

> PTSD is a disorder involving dysregulation of the stress response system, and one of the most powerful effects of yoga is to work on cognitive and physiological stress. What we believe is happening, is that through the control of attention on a target—the breath, the postures, the body—that kind of awareness generates changes in the brain ... and these changes in thinking focus more in the moment, less in the past, and it quiets down the anxiety-provoking chatter going on in the head. People become less reactive and the hormone-related stress cycle starts to calm down.[57]

Currently, a special type of yoga developed especially for people with PTSD is being used therapeutically in dozens of military bases and military hospitals. It focuses on breathing exercises, instruction in meditation and relaxation techniques, and relaxing postures that relieve tightness in the neck, jaw, shoulders, and back—all places where tension tends to build up. To ease the participants' anxieties, the sessions are held in a secure setting in which noises and other factors that can trigger a bad reaction are screened out. This makes it easier for individuals to focus their attention inward and relax, rather than worrying about external threats.

Yoga and Sleep

One important way yoga helps people with PTSD is by improving the quality of their sleep. Indeed, research indicates that practicing yoga helps solve sleep problems for everyone. There are multiple ways yoga affects sleep. First, sleep onset is linked to an increase in activity in the parasympathetic nervous system. Therefore, by enhancing activity in the parasympathetic nervous system, yoga helps encourage sleep. Practicing yoga also promotes sleep by increasing the production of serotonin and melatonin, two neurotransmitters that induce sleep and help regulate the sleep-wake cycle. Researchers have not yet learned why this occurs but theorize that the production of these neurotransmitters is linked to the parasympathetic nervous system.

Secondly, while all forms of physical activity promote a good night's sleep by tiring the body, yoga is one of a few forms of exercise that focuses on reducing muscle tension, which promotes good sleep. Individuals can sleep with tense muscles but doing so affects the quality of sleep. It can cause muscle pain and cramps during sleep and headaches, jaw, back, shoulder, or neck pain upon awakening.

Finally, many individuals who have problems falling asleep say they have trouble turning off their mind. They are bothered with feelings of anxiety, including worries

The Special Yoga Center in London, England, conducts a demonstration of yoga nidra, which is said to be a remedy for insomnia.

about not being able to sleep. By teaching individuals ways to calm themselves through deep breathing and how to let go of negative thoughts and focus their attention inward, yoga helps people shut off their minds, reduce anxiety, and fall asleep.

To examine yoga's impact on sleep, a 2012 Harvard Medical School study considered how daily yoga practice might affect the sleep of individuals with insomnia. In this study, twenty subjects practiced yoga daily for eight weeks. The subjects kept sleep logs for two weeks before they began practicing yoga and for the duration of the study. They recorded the amount of time they slept per night, the number of times they awakened during the night, and other details about their sleep. At the close of the study, the subjects all recorded increased sleep time and improved ability to fall asleep and stay asleep. Other studies have reported similar results. As Khalsa explains, "Yoga is an effective treatment because it addresses insomnia's physical and psychological aspects."[58]

Developing Healthy Habits

Getting adequate sleep is just one important health habit that yoga promotes. Yoga also helps people avoid or break unhealthy habits such as overeating, smoking, and/or alcohol or substance abuse. Individuals often turn to unhealthy habits to deal with stress, anxiety, depression, low self-esteem, and other negative feelings. Practicing yoga, with its focus on mindfulness, body awareness, breath control, and being nonjudgmental helps individuals gain control of the negative emotions that lead to unhealthy habits. These same factors also influence individuals to make healthier choices, while yoga's stress-reducing qualities make it easier to break bad habits triggered by stress.

Yogic body awareness gives some smokers the desire to quit. Through yogic breathing, they become more conscious of their breathing and the way smoking negatively affects their respiration. That is what happened to blogger India Hope, who explains: "When I started the amazing practice of yoga I quickly realized the importance of breath. I did

EFFECTS OF SYMPATHETIC AND PARASYMPATHETIC STIMULATION

Organ	Effect of Sympathetic Stimulation	Effect of Parasympathetic Stimulation
Heart	Increased rate, increased force of contraction (of whole heart)	Decreased rate, decreased force of contraction (of atria only)
Blood Vessels	Constriction	Dilation of vessels supplying the penis and clitoris only
Lungs	Dilation of bronchioles (airways), inhibition of mucus secretion	Constriction of bronchioles, stimulation of mucus secretion
Digestive Tract	Decreased motility (movement), contraction of sphincters (to prevent forward movement of contents), inhibition of digestive secretions	Increased motility, relaxation of sphincters (to permit forward movement of contents), stimulation of digestive secretions
Urinary Bladder	Relaxation	Contraction (emptying)
Eye	Dilation of pupil, adjustment of eye for far vision	Constriction of pupil, adjustment of eye for near vision
Liver (glycogen stores)	Glycogenolysis (glucose released)	None
Adipose Cells (fat stores)	Lipolysis (fatty acids released)	None

Source: Austin Community College, "Effects of Parasympathetic and Sympathetic Divisions on Various Organs," Peripheral Nervous System–Efferent Division (Autonomic and Motor). http://www.austincc.edu /apreview/PhysText/PNSefferent.html.

not really have an issue during my practice with breathing, I wasn't 'out of breath' the whole time but I could tell something was not allowing me to release and let go like my mind, body and spirit wanted me to. I felt constricted. I knew at this moment I wanted to quit."[59]

MEDITATE

72.2%

Percentage of U.S. yoga practitioners who are female, according to a 2013 *Yoga Journal* report. 27.8 percent are male.

Many smokers say that stress causes them to smoke. Yoga's stress-fighting ability gives smokers a tool to counter stress so they can quit. In a 2013 Indian study, a group of smokers received advice on quitting as well as training in using yogic breathing as a tool to quit smoking. A control group received just the advice. A month later, 77 of the 574 people in the yoga group had quit smoking compared to 41 of the 586 people in the control group. This constituted about a 50 percent difference, indicating the value of yogic breathing in helping individuals stop smoking.

Mindfulness also helps individuals break unhealthy habits. Mindfulness teaches individuals to recognize negative thoughts and move past them. This, according to British yoga teacher Marion Ancker:

Results in suspending judgment and being able to observe negative feelings and thoughts (even cravings) without emotional response. Therefore, you feel less caught up in your thoughts as you just observe them come and go. This cultivates a more balanced perspective, which is key to overcoming addiction [and unhealthy habits], and it also allows people to forgive themselves. Past behaviours can be acknowledged without guilt or self-punishment and mistakes seen in perspective. This allows people to move on from addiction.[60]

Mindfulness also teaches individuals to be in the moment. This is helpful to overeaters who often eat to escape what they are feeling, and therefore eat so quickly and mindlessly that they disassociate from their bodies and do not notice how much they are eating, the taste of the food, or whether they feel full. Mindfulness helps them to slow down, savor each bite, and be more conscious of their physical state. "There's this sense that I have to feel better right now," explains Maggie Juliano the director of Sprout Yoga, an organization that uses yoga to help people with eating disorders. "You have no connection to what you're eating. You're eating a pint of ice cream and can't even taste it. . . . The whole point of yoga is to stay connected to your body. You learn it through practice, through breathing, and through breathing through the sensations."[61]

A 2010 Australian study examined yoga's effect on a group of obese women who battled with binge eating. The subjects attended one hour-long yoga class per week for twelve weeks and practiced yoga for thirty minutes a day at home. Yoga practice included asanas, breathing exercises, and meditation. All of the components emphasized mindfulness. At the close of the study, the subjects reported less binge eating and more positive self-esteem. The subjects also showed a decrease in their body mass index and in their waist and hip measurements.

Concentration and Memory

Yoga not only appears to lift moods and emotions, improve sleep, and encourage healthful habits, but a growing body of evidence indicates that yoga enhances concentration and memory as well. Yoga impacts concentration and memory both psychologically and physiologically. Research indicates that psychologically, yoga practitioners seem to be able to transfer the skill of focusing their attention and tuning out distractions that they learn through yoga to other activities, thereby improving their overall power of concentration. A 2013 University of Illinois, Urbana, study investigated whether twenty minutes of yoga practice could improve a group of college students' speed and accuracy on a test of memory. The subjects did Hatha yoga for one twenty-minute session and walked on a treadmill for another session. Following each session, the subjects were administered a memory test. Then their scores were compared. The subjects' test scores were higher after practicing yoga than after walking. "It appears that following yoga practice, the participants were better able to focus their mental resources, process information quickly, more accurately and also learn, hold and update pieces of information more effectively than after performing an aerobic exercise bout," lead researcher

Neha Gothe explains. "The breathing and meditative exercises aim at calming the mind and body and keeping distracting thoughts away while you focus on your body, posture or breath. Maybe these processes translate beyond yoga practice when you try to perform mental tasks or day-to-day activities."[62]

Physiologically, yoga's power to relieve stress and anxiety also boosts concentration and memory. These emotions interfere with a person's ability to concentrate and lead to forgetfulness. In fact, some schools that have instituted daily yoga practice report an increase in student performance and alertness. Also physiologically, research using brain imaging has shown that yoga increases blood flow to the *pre-frontal cortex*, the part of the brain that influences attention, concentration, and memory. As a result, the pre-frontal cortex gets the nutrition it needs to function optimally, which in turn improves concentration and memory.

Changing the Brain

Increased blood flow to the pre-frontal cortex is not the only physical impact yoga has on the brain. Research has shown that the brain is constantly growing, changing, and remodeling itself as a result of experience. As a result, the more often an action is repeated, the greater the growth and change. The ability of the brain to grow and change is known as *neuroplasticity*. Scientists think that neuroplasticity is involved in all kinds of learning, sensory perception, and emotions. The brain, explains neuroplasticity expert Michael Merzenich of the University of California at San Francisco, "[Is] a machine that's constantly remodeling itself based on how you use it. When we start to lose our cognitive abilities, it's not so much a problem of the brain's physical condition but a result of how it's been used."[63]

Learning various yoga practices promotes neuroplasticity. It stimulates the brain to create new neural pathways that allow neurons to connect with each other. The more often individuals practice yoga, the greater the number of these connections, and the larger and stronger they become. According to McCall, "When you study yoga, you are learn-

A man who suffers progressive cognitive impairment practices yoga at his home in Washington, D.C., as a way to battle the disease.

ing completely new ways to move the body, and coordinating different actions simultaneously. Beyond all the variety of asana, there are breathing techniques, mantras, and different kinds of meditation. Each of these activities causes the brain to build new synapses, the connection between neurons."[64]

Although all forms of exercise appear to enhance neuroplasticity, yoga seems to be especially effective. This may be because yoga integrates mind, body, and breath, so it stimulates the brain on many levels. Researchers at Massachusetts General Hospital, Boston, have conducted a number of studies in which they used brain imaging to assess the impact of yoga on the structure of the brain. For example, in a 2010 study, the researchers taught sixteen subjects yoga postures and mindful meditation, which the subjects practiced for approximately thirty minutes a day for eight weeks. Two weeks before the study began, the researchers took magnetic resonance images (MRI) of the subjects' brains as well as those of a control group. After eight weeks, another set of images were taken. Then the images were compared. The brains of the yoga group showed significant increases in neuron density in two important parts of the brain—the *hippocampus*, which is involved in learning and emotional regulation, and the *parietal lobe*, which is involved in compassion and self-awareness. The brains of the control group showed no measurable changes.

Another brain imaging study conducted by researchers at McGill University, Toronto, in 2013, investigated whether yoga practice had any structural effect on the parts of the brain involved with tolerating pain. In this study, researchers immersed the hands of fourteen long-term yoga practitioners and fourteen individuals who never practiced yoga in ice cold water until the subjects could no longer tolerate the pain. On average, the yoga group tolerated pain twice as long as the other subjects. The researchers also took brain images of both groups. They found that the parts of the brain involved in pain processing and regulation, and the parts of the brain involved in general attention were denser in the yoga group than those of the non-yoga group. Moreover, the volume of density correlated with the length of time the subjects had been practicing yoga. The researchers do not know why yoga practice affects the structure of the parts of the brain involved with pain regulation. However, they observed that the yoga practitioners used yogic strategies such as breath control and focused their attention inward to help them tolerate the cold water, while the control group did not. Based on their observations and the brain images, they concluded that practicing yoga gives individuals tools that help them deal with pain, and repeated use of these tools changes the structure of the brain. Commenting on the results of these and other studies, Dharma Singh Khalsa, yoga practitioner and the president and medical director of the Alzheimer's Research and Prevention Foundation, concludes, "This is evidence that you can move beyond molding and shaping the mind: You can literally create a new brain. It's beyond neuroplasticity. It's neurogenesis [the creation of new nerve cells]."[65]

Whether or not practicing yoga can actually stimulate the creation of new nerve cells remains to be investigated. Modern science is just beginning to discover all the beneficial effects of this ancient discipline. Physiology, biomechanics, physics, chemistry, and psychology all figure prominently in yoga. But it is the feeling of mental and physical well-being that yoga imparts that motivates yoga practitioners all over the world.

NOTES

Chapter 1: An Ancient Practice

1. "General Yoga Information." American Yoga Association. www.ameri canyogaassociation.org/general .html.
2. Georg Feuerstein. "A Short History of Yoga." SwamiJ.com. www .swamij.com/history-yoga.htm.
3. Timothy McCall. *Yoga as Medicine.* New York: Bantam, 2007, p. 10.
4. Quoted in Richard Corliss. "The Power of Yoga." *Time,* April 15, 2001. http://content.time.com/time /health/article/0,8599,106356,00 .html.
5. Timothy McCall. "Yoga Therapy and the Mind-Body Connection, Part 1." *Yoga Journal.* www.yoga journal.com/for_teachers/2621.
6. "Emotions and Health." *NIH Medline Plus,* Winter 2008. www.nlm .nih.gov/medlineplus/magazine /issues/winter08/articles/winter08 pg4.html.
7. William J. Broad. *The Science of Yoga.* New York: Simon and Schuster, 2012, pp. 31–33.
8. T.K.V. Desikachar. *The Heart of Yoga.* Rochester, VT: Inner Traditions International, 1995, p. xxvi.
9. Desikachar. *The Heart of Yoga,* p. xvii.
10. Broad. *The Science of Yoga,* p. 2.

Chapter 2: The Practice of Yoga

11. Suzanne Maguire. "3 Benefits of a Warm-up in Yoga." My Yoga Online, September 2, 2013. www.my yogaonline.com/about-yoga/learn -about-yoga/3-benefits-of-a-warm -up-in-yoga.
12. Leslie Kaminoff and Amy Matthews. *Yoga Anatomy.* Champaign, IL: Human Kinetics, 2012, pp. 45–46.
13. Janet Tsai. "Newton's Third Law: The Spanda of Actions and Reactions." Forces in Yoga, August 19, 2010. http://forcesinyoga.com/blog/?p=14.
14. Tsai. "Newton's Third Law."
15. Georg Feuerstein and Larry Payne. *Yoga for Dummies.* Hoboken, NJ: Wiley, 2010, p. 96.
16. Kreg Weiss. "Yoga and Lines of Gravity." Kreg Weiss Yoga, July 9, 2012. http://kregweiss.ca/2012/07 /09/yoga-and-lines-of-gravity.
17. Quoted in Kofi Busia, ed. *Iyengar the Yoga Master.* Boston: Shambhala, 2007, p. 34.

18. Tsai. "Newton's Third Law."

19. Kaminoff and Matthews. *Yoga Anatomy*, p. 129.

20. Ian Rawlinson. "Breathing in Yoga Postures." Ian and Cindy Rawlinson L.Ac. www.rawlinsonacupuncture.com/article_yoga.html.

21. Desikachar. *The Heart of Yoga*, p. 56.

22. Quoted in Dayna Macy. "Eat Like a Yogi." *Yoga Journal*, June 2008. www.yogajournal.com/lifestyle/2724.

23. Quoted in Macy. "Eat Like a Yogi."

Chapter 3: Functional Fitness

24. Allison Kyle Leopold. "Fitness; 'Functional Fitness' Means Training for Your Real Life." *New York Times*, June 6, 2004. www.nytimes.com/2004/06/06/health/fitness-functional-fitness-means-training-for-your-real-life.html.

25. Quoted in Bob Bader. "Fitness Friday: Working Out for Real Life Functions." Real World Personal Training, January 20, 2011. www.realworldpersonaltraining.com/fitness-friday-working-out-for-real-life-functions.

26. Quoted in Fernando Pages Ruiz. "What Science Can Teach Us About Flexibility." *Yoga Journal*. www.yogajournal.com/practice/209.

27. Quoted in Sharon Tanenbaum. "Increase Your Flexibility and Improve Your Life." *Real Simple*, July 2010. www.realsimple.com/health/fitness-exercise/stretching-yoga/increase-flexibility-improve-life-00000000037981.

28. Nina Zolotow and Shari Ser. "Range of Motion: Yoga's Got it Covered!" Yoga for Healthy Aging, March 2013. http://yogaforhealthyaging.blogspot.com/2013/03/range-of-motion-yogas-got-it-covered.html#!/2013/03/range-of-motion-yogas-got-it-covered.html.

29. Quoted in "Does Increasing Flexibility Help or Hinder Athletic Performance?" Sharecare. www.sharecare.com/health/sports-and-athletic-performance/does-flexibility-help-athletic-performance.

30. Quoted in Leopold. "Fitness; 'Functional Fitness' Means Training for Your Real Life."

31. Quoted in Gina Shaw. "Working Out for Real Life Functions." WebMD, August 12, 2003. www.webmd.com/fitness-exercise/features/working-out-for-real-life-functions?page=2.

32. McCall. *Yoga as Medicine*, p. 38.

33. Deborah Khoshaba. "Take a Stand for Yoga Today." *Psychology Today*, May 23, 2013. www.psychologytoday.com/blog/get-hardy/201305/take-stand-yoga-today.

34. Quoted in Alice G. Walton. "Penetrating Postures, Part II: The Psychology of Yoga." *Forbes*, June 22, 2011. www.forbes.com/sites/alicegwalton/2011/06/22/penetrating

-postures-part-ii-the-psychology
-of-yoga.

35. Quoted in Broad. *The Science of Yoga*, p. 136.

36. Quoted in Joanna Walters. "'Yoga Can Damage Your Body' Article Throws Exponents Off-balance." *The Guardian*, January 14, 2012. www.theguardian.com/lifeand style/2012/jan/14/yoga-can -damage-body-row.

37. Quoted in Broad. *The Science of Yoga*, p. 125.

Chapter 4: Yoga and Physical Health

38. Quoted in Heather Boerner. "Positively Healing." *Yoga Journal*. www .yogajournal.com/health/2587.

39. Quoted in Sheila M. Eldred. "Yoga Changes Gene Expression, Improves Immunity." News Discovery, April 26, 2013. http://news .discovery.com/human/health /yoga-benefits-immune-system -changes-genes-130427.htm.

40. Quoted in "Yoga Improves Respiratory Function." News Medical.net, April 6, 2006. www.news -medical.net/news/2006/04 /06/17144.aspx.

41. Quoted in McCall. *Yoga as Medicine*, p. 185.

42. Quoted in Go Red for Women Editors. "Health Benefits of Yoga." American Heart Association. www .goredforwomen.org/live-healthy /heart-healthy-exercises/health -benefits-of-yoga.

43. Quoted in Catherine Guthrie. "Yoga for Bone Health." *Yoga Journal*, May 2011. www.yogajournal .com/health/2616.

44. Quoted in Ankita Rao. "Dr. Yogi: Physicians Integrate Yoga into Medical Practice." NPR, February 27, 2014. www.npr.org/blogs /health/2014/02/26/283090357 /integrating-yoga-into-medical -practice-its-more-than-just -relaxation-response.

45. Quoted in Nora Isaacs. "Yoga Therapy: The Next Wave in Yoga." GAIAM Life. http://life.gaiam.com /article/yoga-therapy-next-wave -yoga.

46. Quoted in Nora Isaacs. "The Yoga Therapist Will See You Now." *New York Times*, May 10, 2007. www .nytimes.com/2007/05/10/fashion /10Fitness.html?pagewanted=all &_r=0.

47. McCall. *Yoga as Medicine*, pp. 19–20.

48. Julie Gudmestad. "Ease on Back." *Yoga Journal*. www.yogajournal .com/health/125.

49. Quoted in Donna Olmstead. "The Yoga Boost." *Live Well, Albuquerque Journal*, April 2014, p. 8.

50. Quoted in "Yoga Regulates Stress Hormones and Improves Quality of Life for Women with Breast Cancer Undergoing Radiation Therapy." MD Anderson Cancer Center, March 3, 2014. www.md anderson.org/newsroom/news -releases/2014/yoga-regulates -stress.html.

51. Amanda Nixon. "How Breast Cancer Made Me a Yogini." *Huffington Post*, September 29, 2012. www.huffingtonpost.com/amanda-nixon/breast-cancer-yoga_b_1923800.html.

Chapter 5: Yoga and the Mind

52. Quoted in "Yoga for Depression: A Conversation with Amy Weintraub." Levitating Monkeys, December 3, 2013. http://levitating monkey.com/yoga-for-depression-amy-weintraub.

53. Emily Deans. "Evolutionary Psychiatry." *Psychology Today*, March 15, 2013. www.psychologytoday.com/blog/evolutionary-psychiatry/201303/yoga-ba-gaba.

54. McCall. *Yoga as Medicine*, p. 267.

55. "Anxiety." American Psychological Association. www.apa.org/topics/anxiety.

56. Art Matthews. "Why Is Yoga Good for Anxiety?" Choose Help, November 7, 2011. www.choosehelp.com/experts/anxiety/anxiety-arthur-matthews/why-is-yoga-good-for-anxiety.

57. Quoted in Rachel Zimmerman. "Harvard, Brigham Study: Yoga Eases Veterans' PTSD Symptoms." Common Health, December 8, 2010. http://commonhealth.wbur.org/2010/12/harvard-brigham-medical-study-yoga-veterans-ptsd.

58. Quoted in Elaine Gavalas. "Yoga Helps Relieve Sleep Problems." *Huffington Post*, October 12, 2012. www.huffingtonpost.com/elaine-gavalas/yoga-sleep_b_1719825.html.

59. India Hope. "How Yoga Helped Me Quit Smoking." Mind Body Green, August 16, 2012. www.mindbodygreen.com/0-5831/How-Yoga-Helped-Me-Quit-Smoking.html.

60. Marion Anckler. "Overcoming Addiction and Bad Habits with Yoga." Yoga Circle. www.yogacircle.co.uk/overcoming_addictions.html.

61. Quoted in Kelly McGonigal. "How Yoga Can Help End Binge Eating." *Psychology Today*, July 4, 2010. www.psychologytoday.com/blog/the-science-willpower/201007/how-yoga-can-help-end-binge-eating.

62. Quoted in Diana Yates. "A 20-Minute Bout of Yoga Stimulates Brain Function Immediately After." News Bureau Illinois, June 5, 2013. http://news.illinois.edu/news/13/0605yoga_EdwardMcAuley.html.

63. Quoted in Hilari Dowdle. "Good Memory." *Yoga Journal*. www.yogajournal.com/health/2576.

64. McCall. *Yoga as Medicine*, p. 40.

65. Quoted in Dowdle. "Good Memory."

GLOSSARY

asanas: Yoga postures.

autonomic nervous system: The part of the nervous system that regulates the function of organs sich as the heart and lungs.

complementary therapy: Medical treatment that combines traditional medical treatments with alternative treatments.

conscious breathing: Awareness of one's breathing.

core muscles: The muscles that surround the spine, chest, and pelvis.

cortisol: A hormone that is released when the body is under stress.

functional fitness: The ability to perform daily activities safely and easily.

gamma-aminobutyric acid (GABA): A neurotransmitter linked to positive mood and emotions.

Hatha yoga: A physical form of yoga that is the basis of most modern yoga practices.

mantra: A word or phrase that individuals repeat in order to calm the mind while meditating.

musculoskeletal system: The body system consisting of the bones, joints, muscles, and connective tissues.

neurotransmitters: Chemicals that allow brain cells or neurons to communicate with each other.

parasympathetic nervous system: The branch of the autonomic nervous system that helps individuals to relax.

pranayama: Yogic breathing exercises.

proprioception: The body's ability to sense its position and movement without a visual guide.

static-active stretching: Stretching a muscle as far as it can comfortably go and then holding the stretch without any assistance.

sympathetic nervous system: The branch of the autonomic nervous system that produces a "fight or flight" response to a perceived threat.

yoga therapy: The use of yoga practices to treat physical or mental health conditions.

Books

David H. Coulter. *Anatomy of Hatha Yoga: A Manual for Students, Teachers, and Practitioners*. Honesdale, PA: Body and Breath, 2010. This book looks at the anatomy and physiology of yoga in scientific terms with lots of illustrations.

Sumukhi Finney. *The Yoga Handbook*. New York: Rosen Classroom, 2009. A yoga manual aimed at teenage women, with photos and directions on how to do different poses.

Sarah Herrington. *Idiot's Guides: Yoga*. New York: Alpha Books, 2013. The book provides instruction on how to do dozens of yoga poses with colored illustrations, practice sequences, and instruction on yogic breathing exercises.

Amie Leavitt. *Yoga Fitness*. Hockessin, DE: Mitchell Lane, 2014. Geared toward young people, this book gives information on different types of yoga, new trends in yoga, and safety information.

Internet Sources

"Autonomic Nervous System." Neuroscience for Kids. http://faculty .washington.edu/chudler/auto .html.

"The Physics of Yoga." Wisconsin Public Television. http://video.wpt.org /video/2123264712.

"Scientific Results of Yoga for Health and Well-Being Video." National Institutes of Health. http://nccam.nih .gov/video/yoga.

Websites

ABC of Yoga (www.abc-of-yoga.com). This website is a portal to information about yoga exercises, styles, apparel, history, news, breathing techniques, and health benefits, with forums, videos, and links.

American Yoga Association (www .americanyogaassociation.org /contents.html). This nonprofit educational organization offers lots of information about yoga on its website, including information on finding a qualified yoga teacher.

Forces in Yoga (www.forcesinyoga.com /pa/Home.html). Engineer and yoga teacher Janet Tsai uses yoga to explain physics and engineering concepts.

Yoga Alliance (www.yogaalliance.org). This nonprofit organization provides information on how to become an accredited yoga instructor, how to find an instructor or yoga therapist, articles on the benefits of yoga, articles on yoga as a business, and many videos.

Yoga Journal (www.yogajournal.com). This is the online version of the *Yoga Journal*, a magazine dedicated to yoga. The website offers dozens of articles on yoga history, poses, meditation, breathing, and yoga and health.

YoMe (http://yogameditationhome.com). This website offers lots of free online instructional videos of different yoga poses, meditation techniques, yoga styles, and videos of yoga classes.

INDEX

Cortisol reduction, 12, 60–61, 73–74, 80–81

D

Desikachar, T.K.V., 22, 23, 38
Downward facing dog, *33*, 50, 56

F

Functional fitness
    aerobic vs. anaerobic, 42–43
    balance and coordination, 27, 50–53, 59
    flexibility and range of motion, 42, 45–49, *46*, *48*, 59, 75
    injuries, *55*, 55–57, *57*
    relaxation benefits, 52–54
    strength and endurance, 48–50, *50*

G

Gentle yoga, 23
Gune, Jagannath, 16–19

H

Hatha yoga, 14–16, 21
History of yoga, 9–12, 16

I

Immune system, 60–62, 74
Injuries, *55*, 55–57, *57*
Inversion poses, *31*, 35, 56–57
Iyengar, B.K.S., *18*, 19–20

J

Jnana (wisdom) yoga, 13

K

Karma (action) yoga, 13
Kid yoga, 23

Knee pain, 42, 69
Kneeling poses, 30, 34–35
Krishnamacharya, Tirumalai, 16–17, 19, 22

L

Let's Move! program, 24
Light on Yoga (Iyengar), 19–20

M

Meditation
    brain wave patterns, 39
    breathing preparation, 8, *36*, 38
    cross-legged posture, 9, *11*, 34, *36*, *39*
    definition, 12, 13
    Mind Over Madness event, *78*
    om mantra, 40
    strategies, 15, 38–39
    yogic chanting, 37
Mental health
    anxiety reduction, 80–82, *81*
    brain neuroplasticity, 90–91
    concentration and memory, 89–90
    cortisol reduction, 12, 60–61, 73–74, 80–81
    healthy habits, 86–89
    moods, 77–80
    pain control, 91–92
    post-traumatic stress disorder, 82–84
    sleep, 84–86
Mind-body connection, 16, 66, 76
Mountain pose *(tadasana)*, 32, 34

N

Natarajasana (Lord of the Dance) pose, *29*

O

Obama, Michelle, 24
Overstretching injuries, 55–56

P

Parasympathetic nervous system
    effects of, 12, 87*t*
    post-traumatic stress disorder and, 83
    yoga's effect on, 38, 53, 61, 66, 85
Patanjali, 12–14
Physical health
    cardiovascular system, 60, *63*, 64–66
    immune system, 60–62, 74
    respiratory system, 12, 60, 62–64, *63*
    skeletal system, 27, 34, 66–67
    See also Yoga therapy
Postures. *See* Asanas
Power yoga, 22, 43
Pranayama. *See* Breath control
Prenatal yoga, 23
Prisons/prisoners, 83, *83*

R

Range of motion and flexibility, 42, 45–49, *46*, *48*, 59, 75
Reasons for practicing yoga, *21*
Relaxation response, 12, 26, 44, 52–54, 61, 73
Respiratory system, 12, 60, 62–64, *63*
Royal (Raja) yoga, 13

S

Seated postures, 9, 34, 59
Skeletal system (bones), 27, 34, 66–67
Sleep, yoga and, 75, 84–86, *85*, 89
Spiritual enlightenment, 9, 13, 14
Standing postures
    benefits, 31
    elderly person study, 67
    mountain pose, 32, 34
    Sun Salutation, 30
    tree pose, 52
    Warrior pose, *29*, 30, 32–33, *43*, 66
Static-active stretching, 27, *28*
Strength and endurance, 48–50, *50*

Stress control, 12
Sun Salutation, 30
Sympathetic nervous system, 12, 53, 61, 64, 83, 87*t*
Systems of yoga, 13–14
    See also individual systems

T

Tantra (Kundalini) yoga, 13–14
Toddler yoga, 23
Twisting poses, 32–36, 42, 45

V

Vegetarian diet, 40–41

W

Warrior pose, *29*, 30, 32–33, *43*, 66

Y

Yoga, early history, 8–12, *9*
Yoga blocks, 19, 57–59
Yoga mats, 57–58, *58*
Yoga practice. *See* Asanas
Yoga straps, 19, 57, 59, 71
Yoga Sutras (Patanjali), 12–14
Yoga teachers
    hands-on approach, 71
    qualifications, 56
    training, 20, 70
Yoga therapy
    back pain, 71–73, *72*
    benefits, 68–69, 75
    as complementary therapy, 68–70, *68*, *69*, *91*
    cancer, 73–76, *74*
    knee pain, 69
    session description, 70–71
    training programs, 67–68

PICTURE CREDITS

Cover: Feng Yu/Shutterstock.com; ©holbox/Shutterstock.com; © wavebreakmedia/Shutterstock.com

© Andrew Errington/Getty Images, 39

© AP Images/Patti Longmire, 83

© AP Images/The Plain Dealer, Marvin Fong, 69

© AP Images/Vino Wong, Atlanta Journal Constitution, 24

© Brian Cahn/ZUMA Press/Newscom, 50

© Cory Richards/National Geographic/Getty Images, 28

© Ed Jones/AFP/Getty Images, 55, 58

© Essdras M Suarez/The Boston Globe/Getty Images, 72

© Frank Bienewald/LightRocket via Getty Images, 66

© Gale, Cengage Learning, 21, 29, 57, 68, 87

© Godong/Universal Images Group via Getty Images, 26

© Howard Sochurek/Time & Life Pictures/Getty Images, 11

© JB Reed/Bloomberg via Getty Images, 74

© Jim Davis/The Boston Globe via Getty Images, 22

© John Moore/Getty Images, 78

© Michael Zagaris/Oakland Athletics/Getty Images, 48

© Mirrorpix/Newscom, 18

© nanka/Shutterstock.com, 61

© National Museum of India, New Delhi, India/Bridgeman Images, 9

© Nick Cunard/ZUMA Press/Newscom, 85

© Nikki Kahn/The Washington Post via Getty Images, 91

© Peter Jordan_NE/Alamy, 33

© Philippe Lissac/Godong/ Newscom, 36

© PM Images/Getty Images, 43

© Ramesh Sharma/India Today Group/Getty Images, 31

© Raminder Pal/SINGH/EPA/Newscom, 63

© Richard MarshallL/KRT/Newscom, 81

© Steve Russell/Toronto Star via Getty Images, 46

© Thomas Northcut/Getty Images, 51

© Wallace Kirkland/Time & Life Pictures/Getty Images, 17

ABOUT THE AUTHOR

Barbara Sheen is the author of eighty-five books for young people. She lives in New Mexico with her family. In her spare time, she likes to swim, cook, garden, lift weights, and practice yoga.